Do the Humanities Have To Be Useful?

Edited by

G. Peter Lepage the Harold Tanner Dean, College of
Arts and Sciences

Carolyn (Biddy) Martin University Provost and Professor
of Women's Studies and German Studies

Mohsen Mostafavi Dean, College of Architecture, Art
and Planning and Arthur L. and Isabel B. Wiesenberger
Professor in Architecture

Cornell University

ISBN: 0-9785514-0-0
Library of Congress Control Number: 2006925441

Cover design by Soulellis Studio
5/06 JCP 1.5M 060400

Contents

Acknowledgements

This publication was made possible through the efforts of many faculty and staff members at Cornell University and with support from the Office of the Provost.

We would like to thank faculty who participated in the first humanities roundtable held at Cornell on May 9, 2005, which launched the ongoing discussions that led to the creation of this collection, as well as faculty who shared their thoughts and ideas in later discussions. They include: Dominic Boyer, Ross Brann, Laura Brown, Susan Buck-Morss, Susan Christopherson, Walter Cohen, Jonathan Culler, Brett de Bary, David M. Feldshuh, Maria Fernandez, Alice Fulton, Sandra Green, Salah Hassan, Martin Hatch, Peter Uwe Hoendahl, Biodun Jeyifo, Dominick LaCapra, Scott MacDonald, Michele Moody-Adams, Timothy Murray, Masha Raskolnikov, Jeffrey Rusten, Phoebe Sengers, Franklin M. Spector, Shawkat Toorawa, and Amy Villarejo. Our thanks also go to Franklin Robinson, the Richard J. Schwartz Director of the Herbert F. Johnson Museum of Art at Cornell; to Sarah Thomas, the Carl A. Kroch University Librarian; and to students Katherine Crocker and Rose Ellen Lessy.

This publication was produced by the staff of the Division of University Communications. We thank Thomas W. Bruce, vice president for university communications; Linda Grace-Kobas, senior director of humanities communications; George Lowery, project manager for humanities communications; and Wendy Kenigsberg, graphic designer, in the Office of Publications and Marketing.

We also thank Leslie J. Burke, executive staff assistant, and Gregory Potter, administrative assistant, in the Office of the Dean of the College of Architecture, Art, and Planning for their fine efforts in organizing discussions and assisting in the production of this book of essays.

The Editors

Preface

Recently there has been a great deal of discussion regarding the state of the humanities, both generally and in the specific context of American research universities. Are the humanities in a state of crisis?

To address this condition of — perhaps legitimate — anxiety, groups of Cornell faculty were invited to participate in a number of roundtable discussions. These discussions only confirmed our initial hunch that, far from being in a state of crisis, the humanities, at least at Cornell, are enjoying a vibrant and productive period. But this reassurance still does not counteract the situation of the humanities within a wider cultural context, where ongoing concerns about their importance and value are having an increasing impact on issues such as funding.

In response to this situation some have stressed the need to consider the relationship of the humanities to the public sphere and in particular to find relevant ways in which the humanities could engage with audiences outside of the academy. Inherent in such recommendations is the assumption that the public at large has to be convinced of the usefulness of the humanities. But do the humanities have to be useful? Perhaps. And if yes, then how?

We offer these essays by Cornell faculty members and students in the hope that they will stimulate discussion on campuses and among the national humanities community.

Mohsen Mostafavi, Dean, College of Architecture, Art, and Planning and Arthur L. and Isabel B. Wiesenberger Professor in Architecture

Do the Humanities Have To Be Useful?

Dominic Boyer

Do the humanities have to be useful? That's an easy one: yes. But it's not a matter of needing to become useful; they are useful already. How and to whom they should be useful are much more difficult questions, and it is probably the prickling anxiety that the humanities aren't greatly useful to that many people that motivated the first question.

But allow me to turn this problem around: how could one argue that the humanities aren't useful? Humanistic scholarship and practice come in so many varieties from philosophy, to linguistics, to art, to music, to writing, to architecture, to literary studies and literary criticism, to humanistic social sciences like anthropology. To put it bluntly, how could we imagine that so many people are engaged uselessly? It certainly doesn't seem that way to them. But, still, I think I understand the question. Even as someone who would identify himself as a humanist, I am perplexed and skeptical about some kinds of humanistic practice. They seem arcane, esoteric, even, dare I say, a bit smug in their genius. Derridean criticism, for example, is not my cup of tea. It makes choices in how it engages both texts and the world that I wouldn't make. But I wouldn't doubt for a moment that it is useful. On epistemological grounds I would say that there are multiple potential methods for engaging texts and the world, that choices are made, practices are elaborated, and voilà we have Derridean criticism as one art among many. The real challenge, as Dilthey saw it, is not how to justify one method over the other, that's easy, but how to guarantee that none of them are trivialized relative to the others. On practical grounds the case seems even clearer. Derridean criticism inspires — not all people, to be sure — but it really inspires some of them, both students and faculty. It's like a little prism of truth through which they can understand something about language, about representation, about the world, that no other prism, whether scholarly or commonplace, allows them to do. It may refract light only partially, it may cast shadows elsewhere, but let's be honest, all humanistic (and scientific) practices do. That's the very nature of expertise itself. Meanwhile, when one thinks of the time, energy, and care that is invested into this kind of criticism, when one listens to the passion and certainty of the true believers, even when one doesn't understand a single sentence, how can one doubt that this is a useful practice? For me, I have exactly the same feeling about these Mars rovers of ours. Intrinsically, I don't find the project all that interesting or worth the expense. But when I listen to the scientists talk about the research, when I see how children are captivated by the images, perhaps dreaming a little of a different future, I am persuaded, this work extends old horizons of human knowledge and opens new ones. Therefore it has its uses, even if I can't pretend to understand them entirely. And, that's really the dilemma, isn't it? That our contemporary academic lives and communities of conversation have become so specialized in certain respects that we have to take the usefulness of our colleagues' practices largely on faith. We have to believe that the passion and care we witness them investing into work that seems obscure and remote to us is genuine, that their work has uses, also very practical uses and persuasive rationales, were we to understand their immediate intellectual environments better.

All very well in the collegial world of the university you might say. But what about those many worlds outside university culture? Should we seek recognition there? Is it important that people in government, in business, on the commons, understand why the humanities are useful? Do they already? Do we need to become better translators and public intellectuals? Again, the answers seem to me to be unequivocally yes. But more because interventions in the public humanities would make us better at what we already do than because the humanities are mired in a desperate crisis of uselessness.

Another question is unavoidable: why do so many of us intuit that the humanities are in crisis? Anxiety, as Lacan once said, is the one affect that doesn't lie. Thus it's not a bad place to begin thinking about what we believe to be true. It seems to me that wondering and worrying about our usefulness has been a companion of humanistic practice for a long time. Likewise there have been many therapeutic interventions to address these worries, none of them entirely successful. The reformation and modernization of European universities in the 19th century, for example, was meant to replace the hegemony of theological faculties, metaphysics, and religious dogma with philosophical faculties and the progress of art, reason, and science. But from the very beginning, the various disciplines contained within the rubric of "philosophy" (the love of wisdom) interpreted art, reason, and science rather differently, whether emphasizing language, personality or history, rationality, experience or imagination. Disagreements and disputes mounted as to which discipline could claim attention to the true soul of human being, indeed creating the first "postmodern crisis" in a subsequently never-ending chain of crises of knowledge. Why? Perhaps because the specialization of scholarly methods and attentions only became more elaborate and institutionalized across the 19th and 20th centuries. Dilthey's magnificent, but impossible, effort to reintegrate the human sciences at the end of the 19th century marks the last serious effort (at least in academic philosophy) to imagine the humanities and sciences as a unified whole around which different disciplines would each organize and integrate their contributions. By the 1920s, the sociology of knowledge had pronounced the collapse of Enlightenment economies of universal truth, leaving us, so it seemed, forever asea in interpretation and correlation, traveling within an archipelago of partial, historical, social knowledges. Thus, the desirability but also the somewhat dissatisfying character of the philosophical explorers of the last quarter of the 20th century like Derrida and Foucault. What wonderful prisms they offer, especially when it comes to confirming our intuitions of the contingent underbelly of modern fantasies of power and knowledge. But, in the end, the philosophy of contingency is also contingent philosophy, offering focused, partial interventions into the problem of truth. Even they cannot escape their conditions of possibility and always alreadys.

So how to explain our anxiety about the present state of the humanities? Here is my partial truth. The specialization of scholarly knowledge and practice is a social fact centuries in the making. It is not a matter, as is sometimes implied, of the self-interest, narrow horizons, or esoteric character of contemporary generations of scholars. Moreover this specialization, so much lamented as an impediment to conversation and exchange within universities, is not entirely negative. Without specialized institutions of research and education, without specialized languages and techniques of truth-making, we would lose a great deal of the contemporary abundance of knowledge and events produced within the humanities and the sciences. Without the degree of specialized attentions and techniques that were achieved in the 19th and 20th centuries, there would surely be no Derridean criticism nor for that matter any Mars rovers. The price we pay for our specialization of labor, however, as Adam Smith and Karl Marx observed so long ago, is the receding horizon of the whole, our experiential sense of how all the productive parts fit together. And that is an anxious situation, this feeling that the unity of "humanity" is receding from the specialized activities of "the humanities," that each of us is working such a small plot with high hedges.

Are the humanities in crisis? The question is actually rather preposterous, but it deserves an answer: no. That is to say, I would wager that there have never been so many people engaged in humanistic practices of one kind or another. And that's a positive sign from my point of view, even if, as in all things, quality varies. But the category "the humanities" is in trouble. Because the very success, abundance, and diversity of humanistic practices has made any of the truth-claims made on its collective behalf very tenuous, very partial indeed. We are fighting an anxious losing battle to keep the category of "the humanities" meaningful instead of celebrating the new horizons possible and probable within the specialized human sciences. I'm not saying "the humanities" must be abandoned, just that we shouldn't worry so much about this peculiar collective subject. When people cease to find art, criticism, music, and anthropology useful or inspiring enough to invest their lives and energies into these practices, then I'll worry. Meanwhile, the best therapy for crisis is to live well.

An Area Studies Perspective

Ross Brann

Do the humanities have to be useful? No doubt some humanists' reflexive response to the question would be a defensive "no." In the abstract and in an ideal intellectual universe, questions of the humanities' utility would be misdirected. We tend to think of our enterprise as intrinsically worthwhile simply because we find it interesting. However, in the marketplace of disciplines and ideas that is the contemporary research university as well as in a society that valorizes what is useful, humanists are obliged to protect their work and preserve their intellectual space by asserting that the humanities are indeed significant, valuable, and useful. Indeed, for their part, humanities undergraduates with an eye on life after commencement frequently engage us in conversation about the "usefulness" of their education.

Many humanists resent having to justify the humanities. Privately we regard questions of relevance as secondary to the pleasures of our intellectual regimen and we recall that such a functional posture would have seemed absurd in the pre-modern world. Until relatively recently all knowledge was regarded as part of a single continuum and the disciplines producing it were seen as interrelated if not always equal in value. Only 50 years ago the humanities occupied a highly esteemed, even central place among the disciplines in the American academy. That is no longer the case. In the present technologically minded intellectual, socioeconomic, and political climate it is time for the partisans and practitioners of the humanities to reclaim their place by articulating a compelling vision for their disciplines in relation to the social sciences and biological, natural, and theoretical sciences.

From the vantage point of area studies in general and Near Eastern studies in particular, to question the usefulness of the humanities seems altogether superfluous. Travel, technology, globalizing economic activity, and commercial interests have brought the whole world into direct and continuous contact with the peoples of the Middle East. Under such circumstances one need not be a culturalist to appreciate that knowledge of Middle Eastern languages, religion, history, and culture serves many important purposes in the contemporary world. Because area studies humanists are frequently called upon to explain the values and practices of other societies, they are arguably more comfortable than some of our humanities colleagues with the idea that what we do is indeed useful.

Area studies humanists also tend to have more opportunities than other colleagues to rub shoulders with social scientists who share their interests in a particular region. We should be thinking expansively in encouraging conversations between humanists and scientists to break down the fault lines between their zones of activity in the university and in society at large. There is an obvious place to begin: humanists who study pre-modern history, society, and culture necessarily encounter scientific thinking because pre-modern learning did not set scientific research off from the other disciplines. On the contrary, literary and religious intellectuals were often scientists themselves. In any case pre-modern science belongs to the history of ideas and can be profitably studied together with other contemporary modes of production, expression, and thought.

What is it exactly that students of Near Eastern studies do that we find so interesting and others find so useful? In the broadest sense we study and interpret Near Eastern culture by analyzing the texts, conceptual elements, and structures of thought, values, materials, and practices of the peoples of the Near East from ancient times down to the present. To put it another way: nowadays most of us embrace Clifford Geertz's totalizing notion of "cultural system" in our critical and interpretative practices. Like all humanists we teach singularly important skills such as critical reading, thinking, and writing, and we reflect on the record — material, visual, and written — that speaks to the conditions and purposes of human life. At the same time we are keenly aware of and bound to challenge current efforts to cast the Middle East, in particular Islam, as the site of an overdetermined cultural identity. Following Jean-François Bayart (*The Illusion of Cultural Identity*, University of Chicago Press, 2005), we are resolved to contest the very notion of a stable cultural identity that supposedly informs all of the region's political conflicts and socio-economic cleavages.

The study of Near Eastern languages has long been the essential method for preserving and recovering the traditions of the past and for resituating them in the present (Hans Ulrich Gumbrecht, *The Powers of Philology*, University of Illinois Press, 2003). Indeed, the entire area studies enterprise begins with philology. As Frantz Fanon put it, "to speak a language is to take on a world, a culture." But area studies no longer ends with philology. Rather Near Eastern studies is decidedly interdisciplinary and, at its best, comparatist in approach. We are drawn to analysis of the interplay between society and culture whether we study Near Eastern history, texts, artifacts, or traditional practices. Alongside philological rigor, the diachronic dimension of the humanities is indispensable in area studies. Consider the following: during the ongoing international debate over publication of Danish cartoons demeaning the Prophet of Islam, one hears the assertion, among other things, that Muslim culture is "humorless." To the pre-modern Arabic literary historian such a characterization is preposterous and laughable in view of the abundance of brilliant humor in the literary tradition's poetry, artistic prose, and historical anecdotes. Similarly, could one honestly hope to comprehend the depth of ethnic and religious divisions and political rivalries in post-Saddam Iraq without understanding the varieties of Islam or the imprint and legacy of modern colonialism in the region?

Ironically, Near Eastern studies has never been regarded as more useful than it is today. We are nevertheless deeply ambivalent about some of the attention our venture currently receives and the sense in which it is deemed useful. Influential American political elites tend to treat the region as little more than a zone of internal and external conflict, and they look to our ranks for confirmation of their attitudes or for providing them with the next generation of linguistically prepared policy analysts. Scholars of Near Eastern studies are appreciated for the latter but suspect for challenging the former, especially when we offer nuanced and complex explanations for the region's problems instead of sweeping and often ideologically grounded generalizations. We would prefer to educate our students and the public about the role of the Near East as a bridge between civilizations from time immemorial, about the sustained historical conversation (as well as contest) between Jews, Christians, and Muslims, and about the enduring significance of Islamic humanism and Muslim thinkers and scientists between late antiquity and early modernity. Under such troubling circumstances is it any wonder that humanists are skittish when asked to reflect on the usefulness of our enterprise?

Twenty-first Century Humanities at the Core of the University

Laura Brown, Dominic Boyer, Brett de Bary, and Jane Fajans

At the dawn of the twenty-first century, the humanities face challenges no less urgent than those that led the founders of Cornell to envision a revolutionary transformation of existing institutions of higher education. Our faculty and student bodies themselves are fully the product of a new era of intensified global movement and interconnectedness. Perceptions of culture and value that framed and unified liberal arts curricula in earlier periods can no longer be assumed. Methods of textual transmission and the archiving and dissemination of knowledge that have long been the purview of humanistic scholars are being revolutionized in ways that have repercussions for every level of the life of the university. The modes in which our students perceive the world, receive and process information, and research and analyze it are, without question, in flux. The content, media, and manner of enjoying what we still may call the "work of art" continue to evolve rapidly, not the least when art insists on an intense engagement with technology. Such new productions, and the radical questions of meaning they pose, are still barely addressed in university curricula.

An ambitious envisioning of the humanities should be a process of innovation and renewal. In different historical periods (and granting, of course, that the definition of the humanities has itself undergone transformation historically) the humanities have been invigorated by the challenge of the new. With their commitment to raising questions of meaning, the humanities have often opened spaces for new modes of expression and the recognition of previously marginalized areas of human experience. At the same time, such moments of transformation have also involved fresh recognition of that which is specific to humanistic inquiry — to its fostering of basic capacities of critical thought and expression for which there should be no instrumental justification.

In both the above senses, we propose a renewal of the humanities at the core of the university. Investment in the humanities is urgently needed to enable humanities faculty to be more productive, and to contribute, in nationally recognized ways, to debate on the future of the humanities. Production of a new generation of humanists will not simply involve superficial interdisciplinarity based on the combination of existing competencies. It must provide for the more time-consuming and rigorous training needed to produce new humanists able to engage, for example, twenty-first century interfaces between highly differentiated linguistic and cultural traditions brought into contact through globalization, between philosophy and science, or between computer sciences and the study of music and visual arts.

Renewing the humanities means recognizing that the humanities are at the center of the intellectual and educational mission of the university. In this sense, we might speak of the humanities as a foundation or a core. These terms can have different meanings and associated values. "Foundation" can imply that the humanities provide basic instruction upon which other learning depends and that commitment to this instruction is stable, steady, and unchanging. In the most concrete sense, work in the humanities contributes to the university through:

- the teaching of critical thinking;
- the teaching of many of the basic skills of literacy, including visual and aural literacy and language skills;
- raising and attempting to resolve questions of value;
- raising questions of aesthetics, art, and pleasure relevant to human creativity;
- the teaching of history, the relation between present and past that is a form of self-location; and
- the teaching of cultural legacies from the past that are part of the common heritage of humanity.

Insofar as imparting these basic skills is fundamental to the pedagogical mission of the university, maintaining rigorous instruction in the humanities is integral to the progress of other academic fields.

Locating the humanities at the "core" of the university also suggests that the humanities permeate critical thinking and engage with most, perhaps all, aspects of knowledge production. Concerns about life, wisdom, survival, transformation, and interaction have long been deeply embedded in the humanities. Although the methods of interrogation change from generation to generation, questions about the mysteries of life, the human trajectory, the relations between humans and nature, the quest for understanding of the universe and world we inhabit are ongoing. Those of us who are engaged in understanding the queries and answers to such conundrums in the past and in cultures other than our own are particularly well situated to help interrogate the examinations of these issues in our present context. We can use history, philosophy, literature, ethnography, and critical reasoning to examine the array of perspectives and answers our forebears have provided. We can use these same tools to examine the way questions are framed in the current context. Most importantly, we can use our critical capacities to help us interpret and contextualize the significance of the information we amass towards solving the problems of the future.

One of the issues contemporary societies face is to understand how our domains of knowledge are expanding almost exponentially, while our ability to process and control this knowledge has not kept pace. This is a serious challenge, both for research and for democracy. We might almost say the ability to access the great arenas of knowledge has decreased. Disciplines typically require ever greater degrees of specialization. Our knowledge of matters outside our own arenas often recedes to the lowest common denominator. We must think about how to maintain the connections and expansions of knowledge that enrich the uses to which knowledge can be applied. Similarly, we see the dangers that ready availability of information, but insufficient means of judgment, leads to in much student work where information is gathered from the Internet without understanding the criteria by which scholars judge the work of others and address issues of context, authorship, and critical understanding. These issues are only accelerated at the societal level, in the difficulty of sustaining an informed citizenry. We maintain that these skills are foundational but also "core." A great research university must not only produce knowledge but explore the meanings, ramifications, and dissemination of that knowledge.

If the humanities engage with virtually all aspects of knowledge production, the humanities are then inherently interdisciplinary. Indeed, German modernizers of the European university argued that an intense, principled orientation to the foundational and universal dimensions of knowledge ought to be the highest ideal of the university. When the first generation of American reformers of higher education returned from their European travels to the United States, it was this vision of the university of *Wissenschaft* that informed their efforts to create the first generation of American research universities. Since then, the emergence of social science and, after World War II, the partnership of big government and big science, along with the democratization of higher education, have radically transformed these universities and humanistic study along with them. But technological developments are not the most significant and decisive forces with which humanity is currently grappling, and the sciences alone are not capable of delivering the most compelling solutions to the opportunities and dilemmas posed by the new technologies.

The concerns of nineteenth-century university reformers might still be well-heeded today. For the university to fulfill its public mission, specialized research and research-orientations must be offset by a disciplined, rigorous pursuit of the wholeness of human knowledge. The humanities must remain basic to the highest aspiration of a research university, the dimension of intellectual life that seeks expressly to connect the myriad activities and achievements of the university back to the collective and public interests of society as a whole. Through the humanities' central commitment to finding the universal in the particular, and vice-versa, we are particularly well-placed to restore a sense of proportion to new scientific and technological developments. The last three decades have witnessed, to be sure, wondrous technological developments, yet other dimensions of human life have been changing as well, often in less spectacular but equally significant ways. Universities must take the lead in supporting humanistic activities that either make dialogues more accessible to the public or seek to deepen the capacity of the humanities to inform the evolution of public culture in its new forms.

Humanistic Explanation

Walter Cohen

Among the paradoxes bedeviling the humanities today is the increasing apparent relevance of the areas of humanities research and teaching, which are not confined to high culture to nearly the extent they were 40 years ago, coupled with the perception often shared by humanists, other academics, and the public that the humanities are less influential or more out of touch with ordinary concerns than ever. Of interest here is the sense that in trying to be useful, the humanities have become useless, and this is decried either as a missed opportunity or as the consequence of a failure to understand that the humanities shouldn't have been messing with utility (read: progressive politics) in the first place.

Now, if utility is defined broadly, of course the humanities ought to be useful; if it is defined narrowly, of course they need not be. But lack of necessity is not the same as lack of opportunity, and I will claim that although there are compelling reasons for much humanistic work not to strive for or achieve utility, some humanists can contribute something that is important but otherwise unavailable. I've put this broadly so as to allow for various possible ways of giving content to the assertion. Here's mine.

Though most humanists do not regularly think in these terms, there is only one credible explanatory account of the last half millennium and that is the development of capitalism seen as centrally related to a whole series of other changes, including the Protestant Reformation, the formation of the nation-state and the rise of nationalism, European global imperialism, the development of modern science and the Industrial Revolution, the spread of liberal democracy, the (ultimately defeated) challenge of socialism and Communism, the formal success of anticolonialism, the recent rise of (anti)globalization, and, more generally, the phenomena of modernization and (post)modernity. This interpretive framework is in fact shared across the political spectrum. Against a reductively economic model, of course, many people have emphasized the relative autonomy of culture, and have talked about the ways effects — e.g. culture as a consequence of economic system — can themselves become causes.

But what if even this modified capitalist hypothesis has sometimes obscured a stronger alternative — the argument that culture is a major force in world affairs with significant explanatory weight, in much the same way that one makes the case for economics, politics, technology (including military technology), social structure, and the like? We would then reject the traditional distinction between the sciences (including the quantitative social sciences), which are said to aim at explanation, and the humanities (and interpretive social sciences), which are supposed to focus instead on understanding. The argument would be that the humanities also have a major role in explanation and not just of cultural matters.

This opportunity probably has always been there. In the post-Communist era, however, religious belief has assumed an importance in world affairs surely related to economic matters but utterly transcendent of its noncultural conditions of possibility. Religion is only the most prominent phenomenon. Imputed class interests often tell us little about the political behavior of workers in the industrialized world; cultural analysis might have more to offer. And it would be useful to reassess the new social movements from the same perspective.

There are certainly precedents for this approach — for instance, in accounts of postmodernism and the performativity of gender. Many of these are hampered, however, by their tendency either to fall back on explanations based on economics and social class or to look exclusively for progressive resistance to repressive modes of the dominant culture. Perhaps we would benefit by instead insisting on the explanatory power of culture while rejecting the notion that its effects are necessarily beneficent (or malevolent).

Such an enterprise might result in a substantial intellectual contribution to the analysis of both present and past, it might foster a shared sense among humanists and non humanists alike of the integral role of the humanities in the advance of knowledge, and accordingly it might reduce humanists' aggressive defensiveness and increase their sense of dignity.

Let me provide a historical example. One of the distinctive features of (primarily Western) European history is the formation of a competitive system of states. How did this arise?

The imperial military might of ancient Rome geographically extended the everyday use of Latin to previously Celtic cultures and eventually resulted in the emergence of the Romance languages. But medieval western Europe, or Latin Christendom, was not confined to these boundaries. It came to include Celtic, Slavic, and above all Germanic territories as well, partly through military conquest but primarily through religious missions. In the Latinized lands, the derivation of the vernacular from the learned language impeded the development of a written vernacular. Elsewhere, however, the example of Latin letters inspired vernacular literacy centuries earlier. This linguistic distinctiveness, both oral and written, in turn contributed to the crystallization of separate political structures and in time of modern nation-states.

Thus the Carolingian and Holy Roman Empires proved fragile affairs, but a larger decentralized system remained that combined competition with cooperation. As a result, if a skill or accomplishment could find no further outlet in its indigenous region, it could be taken over and improved upon elsewhere. The heliocentric revolution was the work of a Pole, but further advances came from Italy, Germany, Denmark, and England. Italian and Portuguese sailors led Spanish voyages of discovery and conquest; a Dutch sailor did the same for England. Relatedly, the alphabetic transcription of written language smoothed the path to vernacular literacy, thereby enabling a connection between scientific intellectuals and artisans that facilitated technological innovation.

The implicit comparison here is to China, where the common Sinitic background of the many different languages of the country precluded durable development of more than a single written vernacular, initially rooted in the needs of the state bureaucracy. The historical continuity and geographical unity of China can easily be overstated; nonetheless, the contrast with Western Europe is real enough. Again, the relatively greater difficulty of mastering Chinese characters perhaps impeded an artisan-intellectual link. All this may or may not help answer a controversial question: why did Europe modernize before China, which as late as 1400 was way ahead? But the religious and linguistic interaction outlined above surely explains some of the distinctiveness of European history.

Up to a point, this hypothesis invites testing, for example by comparison of scientific development and literacy rates in Western Europe and China or of Western Europe's competitive state system with that of northern India. Most important, however, many more such hypotheses are potentially accessible but only if you make explanation of the effect of culture on society a serious enterprise within the larger body of humanistic research.

Imagine a World in Which There Is Only Fact

Katherine Crocker

As a double major, I'm not terribly unique, but as a Chemistry and English major, I'm fairly unusual. "Why," asked a brilliant chemistry professor of mine, "why would you ever want to major in English? So you can flip burgers? So you can take out the trash?" Unfortunately, this is the attitude of many scientists towards the humanities in general, a "What have you done for me lately?" mentality that refuses to believe that there's any appreciable worth in studying the humanities.

As the media and the advertising industry constantly remind us, we live in an increasingly technological age. The newest science constantly revises everything from fad diets to arch supports, and scientific research is cited in each case.

In the midst of this beeping, battery-operated, calorie-counting fervor, it's easy to lose perspective: even in the intellectual community found at Cornell University it's easy to find those who assume that science is superior to the humanities, that the humanities are as useless to humanity's wellbeing and progress as an umbrella is to an alligator.

Obviously, my chemistry professor is mistaken in believing that anything without quantifiable reasoning is useless. He has paintings in his office and listens to music while writing his papers; I pointed this out to him, and he, being a fair man and a scientist, admitted that his view was something on the order of ignorant and prejudiced.

Thinking further about our argument, though, I decided that if science is the expression of our ability as humans to reason in extraordinarily complex ways, then the humanities are our equally intrinsic, utterly valuable appreciation of beauty, compassion, and nonscientific contemplation. I tried to think of a world without the humanities: no music, no museums, no concerts, no paintings, no statues, no literature, and no theater. Language, our means of communication and thought, would be precise but lack feeling and intensity.

Perhaps this strikes me as a tragedy only because I am an English major. But as a student of Chemistry's hard logic, I propose that the logical extension of a belief in the superiority of hard fact and science would be to teach predominantly math, science, and engineering at every level. In his book *Hard Times*, Charles Dickens presents a caricature of this practice that is Orwellian at best: "We hope to have, before long, a board of fact, composed of commissioners of fact, who will force the people to be a people of fact, and of nothing but fact... You must use [for all] purposes, combinations [of] mathematical figures which are susceptible of proof and demonstration."

I can't imagine a world in which there is only Fact: there would be no cultural common ground, no comics in the newspaper. Because everyone who was not making brilliant scientific breakthroughs would be taking out the trash, it would be a clean world — clean to the point of sterility. Without the humanities, we as a society would be unable to bridge cultural gaps, we would be cripples in today's increasingly global society.

Without the humanities, then, our actions would be governed by the black, white, and "very close to the line" that defines quantified reasoning. Without gray areas and multiple right answers, would there be compassion in the world? Would everything be divided into "right" and "wrong," the categories differing in a statistically significant manner? The richness of our beliefs, the spirit of the law, the gut instinct towards kindness — would these things survive if the humanities did not exist? I submit that they would not.

"That's all very well," says my professor, partisan to the end, "but you can't deny that science is more practical than the humanities." I can, and I will. In fact, it's the reason I'm majoring in two such disparate fields: I believe that I would be as crippled without the humanities as I would without science. English keeps my mind open to the qualitative, reminds me to appreciate the paradoxical, amorphous aspects of life. Science requires that I maintain a habitual and very high standard of proof in my reasoning and in understanding qualitative and quantitative ideas. The disciplines pull me in different directions, but the tension keeps my mind from shriveling, keeps me ready to absorb all I can, and perhaps most importantly keeps me from dismissing either camp in its entirety. For me to attempt a balanced life without either would be tremendously impractical, and I think I'm not a bad microcosm of society in this respect.

Science is useful, necessary, and even heartbreakingly beautiful, both in itself and in what it enables us to accomplish. Its uses are obvious. But our reliance on the scientific lulls us, makes us forget that other things with less obvious uses are just as important.

Do the humanities have to be useful? In every culture, by nature of our very existence, we have made them useful, because we cannot survive without them. We were touched by music before we knew it could make us smarter, we haven't always told stories only for their morals, and we don't love one another merely to perpetuate the human race. It's right to take a fierce pride and joy in our scientific advances, and no less right to foster a strong appreciation for the arts and stories. It's right to challenge each other with hard questions and right to defend our own fields, but it's wrong to err on the side of the obvious and forget the necessity of beauty, discounting books simply because they haven't got equations.

"Poetry makes nothing happen"

Jonathan Culler

This famous line of W.H. Auden's comes — ironically yet appropriately — from one of his most political poems, "In Memory of W.B. Yeats (d. Jan. 1939)," which was written on the eve of World War II: "In the nightmare of the dark/All the dogs of Europe bark." Poetry, the poem tells us, "makes nothing happen" but "it survives,/ A way of happening, a mouth." And, putting its money where its mouth is, the poem concludes with solemn, incantatory quatrains, urging the poet to confront the worst, but

> With your unconstraining voice
> Still persuade us to rejoice;
>
> With the farming of a verse,
> Make a vineyard of the curse.
> Sing of human unsuccess
> In a rapture of distress;
>
> In the desert of the heart
> Let the healing fountain start,
> In the prison of his days
> Teach the free man how to praise.

Auden still found a use for poetry. Can it survive today as a way of happening? Cornell's deeply-mourned poet A. R. Ammons, who died in 2001, won the National Book Award in 1993 for his book length poem, *Garbage*.

> garbage has to be the poem of our time because
> garbage is spiritual, believable enough
>
> to get our attention, getting in the way, piling
> up, stinking, turning brooks brownish and
>
> creamy white: what else deflects us from the
> errors of our illusionary ways, not a temptation
>
> to trashlessness, that is too far off, and,
> anyway, unimaginable, unrealistic:

Garbage is concrete and familiar, unavoidable, reminding us always of transitoriness — even the most obdurate objects have become garbage in the dump. And so it is a spiritual category for our time, one that engulfs everything ("mess with a nice dinner long enough, it's garbage"). Garbage is all the discrete objects in landfills and the most general, realistic name for the transitoriness of people and things — the poem of our time, indeed. This wry, eloquent, colloquial, surprisingly cheerful, even jokey poem strings together all sorts of material in long sentences continued by one colon after another (seldom a period in this 100-page poem; all flow rather than structure). These colon sequences are cast in unrhymed couplets that provide an expectation of form: you slow down at line endings but the uncompleted sentences pull you forward as the poem flows from page to page.

. The poem begins with a huge garbage dump in Florida:

> the garbage trucks crawl as if in obeisance,
> as if up ziggurats toward the high places gulls
>
> and garbage keep alive, offerings to the gods
> of garbage, of retribution, of realistic
>
> expectation, the deities of unpleasant
> necessities: refined, young earthworms,

This is the modern temple of sacrifice, with the bulldozer operator as the presiding priest, but Ammons insists,

> this is a scientific poem
>
> asserting that nature models values, that we
> have invented little (copied), reflections of
>
> possibilities already here, this is where we came
> to and how we came: a priestly director behind the
>
> black-chuffing dozer leans the gleanings
> and reads the birds

He reads the circling birds like a soothsayer.

The poem, one might say, explores the relation between three systems:

• a scientific model, in which "garbage" is the name of a temporary stage in the endless transformations of matter and energy. Mass is just a form of energy. Garbage is nothing special, certainly not tragic.

• the redemptive, human model of sacrifice that extracts value, seeks dialectical transumption.

• the process of poetry itself, which is figured as a form of garbage management:

> poetry is itself like an installation at Marine

> Shale: it reaches down into the dead pit
> and cool oil of stale recognition and words and

> brings up hauls of stringy gook which it arrays
> with light and strings with shiny syllables and

> gets the mind back into vital relationship with
> communication channels:

Can poetry mediate between the scientific and the spiritual? Poetry itself is represented as a transmutation of energy:

> there is a mound,

> too, in the poet's mind dead language is hauled
> off to and burned down on, the energy held and

> shaped into new turns and clusters,

The reduction to garbage can yield energy, and this is seen as a form of redemption, as the poem continues

> for

> where but in the very asshole of comedown is
> redemption:...

> where but in the arrangements love crawls us
> through, not a thing left in our self-display

> unhumiliated, do we find the sweet seed of
> new routes:

Yeats noted that "Love has pitched his mansion in the place of excrement," but Ammons's poem denies that such cycles of redemption are a transcendence of nature:

> but we are natural: nature, not
>
> we, gave rise to us:

And poems themselves are seen as concretions of matter, not transcendent but only, on occasion, particularly slow to break down:

> poems themselves
>
> processing, revitalizing so much dead material
> become a dead-material concentrate time's
>
> longest actions sometimes can't dissolve: not
> to worry:

Ironically troping on the idea that poems will outlast gilded monuments, suggesting that they survive only as particularly refractory concentrates of dead matter, this poem, with its remarkable juxtapositions, the intermingling of the high and low, the interweaving of the literary and the scientific, and its astounding inventiveness, could serve us as one modern parable for the humanities, in its negotiation of the meaning of scientific accounts. As it engages the issues of our condition, testing possibilities of thought and evaluative strategies, turning them round, resisting easy lines of escape, does it make something happen? At the very least, Ammons's poem, like Auden's, which is still going strong, survives in the valley of its saying, as a way of happening, offering readers a singular experience and showing us that poems are good to think with.

Against Transparency

Brett de Bary

To respond to a question about the usefulness of the humanities is to negotiate a series of concerns about language that mark the historicity of the humanities at this moment. Who and where are humanists, and what do they have to do with the human? Must we cheerfully announce that the anxiety surrounding this question is a thing of the past? Must we rally to the cause of a sunnier, newer (by all means newer!), ever more inclusive humanities? If we are to remain mindful of the mediality of language, of language as media, can the demand for transparency of language be fully distinguished from a striking intensification of media as surveillance in our time, and from other designs?

To respond to a question about the humanities is first of all to negotiate a question about language. What language to speak? And of course, in what language does one ask the question about language? It is a matter we must not pass over in silence. If the humanities and the human are general terms, in what language do humanists address the human? If one writes in English, whom does one address, and whom does one expect to understand? This is far from a simple matter of relations among what we recognize as modern national language communities. In writing an essay in English about the humanities, for example, does one address one's colleagues in humanities departments (in the United States? elsewhere?), one's graduate students, one's undergraduate students, or a general public? If we must acknowledge (as I have reluctantly in writing this essay) that we do not now have an English language that addresses these different audiences simultaneously, with an equal degree of critical precision, is this a useless observation?

Language inevitably orients us. It does so through its deictic terms, which imply a relationship without specifying referents: its "I"s and "you"s, "here"s and "there"s. In speaking of the humanities today, where is "here" and "there"? Who are "I" and "you"? If there is now no longer a "here" from which to confidently speak as a humanist, from which to orient one's address towards a generality called "the humanities," we must regard this far more as a matter of history than as a result of mistakes made by humanists. The media of a new global order, in familiar and unfamiliar relations to configurations of domination and subjection, homogenize as they fragment. To say that the humanities "no longer has a center," however, is to assume a fixed temporal and spatial framework that is itself the product of just one possible history. What is "lost" or "deconstructed" is seen to be so only from certain perspectives.

This can be said of the "self-critique" carried out by the humanities in European and American universities after 1968, a process deemed "self-destructive" or hyper-reflexive by some anxious cultural commentators then and now. But were those critics, some of whom went so far as to call themselves "anti-humanists" in an effort to undo the boundaries of the human, acted or acted upon? The places from which they wrote had their own long histories as sites of global exchange, of movements of people, forced and unforced. The very description of these processes as "self"-critical seems itself an attempt to perpetuate the notion of a center.

We must acknowledge, then, that the generality called "the humanities" exists in some, but not all, languages and has existed in some, but not all, times. Moreover, the generality we call "the humanities" today must be distinguished from the practice of the people we call humanists. If, from time to time, the practices of those called humanists call into question, reject, transform, or redefine the generality called "the humanities," is this anything new?

Our times call for both hope and reticence on the part of those who would see themselves as humanists. To return to, perpetuate, or reinvent fixed oppositions and anchored perspectives is as fantastical as attempting to deny or transcend our recent history. Our sense of who we are, of who and what we represent, and of our histories themselves is expanding. Not for the first time (and not in the same way everywhere), new media make available information and images at a speed and scale that seem to overwhelm the very perceptual capacities that make us human. It is a time to listen and speak carefully about the human.

Today, amidst shallow banks of snow and chill winds at a university in Ithaca, New York, I — who think of myself as a humanist — walked between two buildings and two conferences. One on popular culture, called "Amusement total….sans regret?!" seemed to allude to the accelerating expansion of perceptual capacities I just mentioned. A paper on hip-hop, to which I listened with interest if not familiarity, argued persuasively that, as sound technologies evolve, it is easier for us to recognize the "presence" of a singular artist in a remix than in an original recording, one using by now outmoded technology. This thoughtful analysis, I reflected, linked technological innovation not with the new but with our sense of the familiar.

A second conference, on "Indigenous Cartographies," brought academics from geography, anthropology, and history departments together with practitioners from indigenous communities around the world. All were involved with the process of "translating" traditional maps to digital ones, done to advance claims for the recognition of lands and cultural monuments by indigenous peoples. In heavy snow the previous day, conferees had arrived from Maine and Managua, from Taiwan and British Columbia, from Ann Arbor and from Fort Defiance, Arizona. For those speakers who addressed the audience in Navajo and Ojibwa, interpreters were provided. The use of GIS, or geographical information systems, I heard, carried promises and risks for indigenous peoples. With digital technologies, boundaries for territorial claims could be delineated in legal disputes more persuasively than in the past. On this basis, the Hul'qumi'num Treaty Group had recently concluded its historic first treaty with the Canadian government. But, as many speakers described, establishing boundaries where none had been before could also lead to conflict. How does one define boundaries in cultures and languages that speak only of land held in common?

Where, I wondered, were the "old" and the "new" in the two discussions I visited? How was I to understand the juxtapositions and convergences of these people and these topics on this snowy day? In Ithaca, New York? What did it mean for me to walk among and between these gatherings and these rooms?

Perhaps what we need at this time is the modesty to recognize that, in the gaps between the generality called "the humanities" and the everyday practices of humanists, the new humanities is already in our midst.

Stories

David Feldshuh

The play was about a hat — a French farce, demanding a deft directorial hand to keep in motion the wit, fluff, and sprinkling of absurd circumstance. I was too young and inexperienced to direct a play that big in one of America's most prestigious theatres, directing some of America's finest actors. But when you're young, you go for the gold. So on a bright late summer day in 1972, I entered the cavernous, dark theatre to chip away at an antique text for those comedic nuggets that might please.

The day was filled with small transgressions: mistakes in front of others, revisions and divisions, small schemes, and jokes that fell flat. And then there were the testings, the tiny battles of will between director and actor, each afraid that their contribution might be slighted or ignored. There is nothing like a bald comedy to reveal failure. If they laugh, you win. Silence, and there's no place to hide. As I finished the eight hours of rehearsal, I had a premonition that this wasn't a story I was born to tell.

A very different story was playing out on a small television at the stage door: the bloodbath of young Israeli athletes and others at the Olympics in Munich, a life-and-death struggle with wide political resonance and profound meaning. After eight hours in the darkness battling to inflate a comedic soufflé, that tiny television screen told an incandescent story that jolted me toward what theatre practitioners call my "superobjective," the spine of your character's life that motivates all the actions: the marriages, the career changes, the adventures, and the cautions. I couldn't even begin to define it at the time. In retrospect, it was simple. Enough soufflé. I wanted to be "useful."

Ten years later, after an intriguing journey through medical school and residency, I was an emergency medicine doctor working a 12-hour shift in a busy metropolitan ER. My next patient, according to the paramedic's radio report, was dead. His story was apparently this: he was working to repair a hydraulic lift at an auto-repair shop when it collapsed, cutting and launching a metal safety rod into his neck. The ambulance arrived within three minutes and found his heart barely beating and his blood pressure dropping. "Asystole," the paramedics radioed a few minutes later. "No pulse." In a crevice of my memory, I recall feeling relieved. Now I knew exactly what I had to do. I had to bring this patient back to life.

I rehearsed twice and then cut along the gentle curve of the sixth rib to allow my hand to reach into this patient's chest and embrace his heart. Reaching into a chest felt like entering a holy place, and I found the heart and let it rest quietly in my hand. Without much hope, I began to squeeze-release, squeeze-release. And then … a quiver. The tips of my fingers felt — or perhaps only sensed — a quiver. I was feeling life restart itself. "We have a pulse," the nurse reported. "Pupils equal and reactive to light." What a beautiful phrase: "equal and reactive to light." And I remember the feeling of pure, adrenalized focus, and, above all, "usefulness." The feeling was unfortunately brief. Six hours later on an operating-room table my patient's heart's stopped again. This time for good.

Shortly after this misadventure, I was thumbing through an issue of the *Journal of the American Medical Association* and found a few lines describing a book by Professor James Jones, called *Bad Blood*. It detailed the story of the so-called "Tuskegee Study." I don't know what motivated me to order the book (hint: my superobjective), but I read and learned about a deceptive United States Public Health Service medical experiment on African-Americans that lasted 40 years and was supervised by seemingly dedicated, caring, and ethical physicians. I began to write a play about the Tuskegee Study motivated by a simple question: "What would I have done as a doctor if I had been asked to join the Tuskegee Study?" That play, much to my surprise, was widely produced at numerous major regional theatres and with stars Laurence Fishburne and Alfre Woodard became an award-winning HBO movie. Most surprisingly, the play and film helped catalyze a change in American history: the apology by President Clinton to the survivors of the Tuskegee Study and the creation of the National Center for Bioethics at Tuskegee University.

The paradox felt embarrassingly obvious. I had left theatre and journeyed into medicine to find something useful, something grounded in society, and now it seems that by the time my life is finished the most "useful" thing I will have accomplished may be the act of writing a play that told a story.

I have always been fascinated by stories, their modesty and their overwhelming efficacy. Surely stories are our oldest teaching tool, and they are abundantly practical across a wide variety of disciplines. In medicine, for example, stories are an antidote to reducing patients to body parts as in, "There's a belly pain in cubicle 4, a headache in 7, and the foot's in 2." Stories reverse this process. As you learn his story, the "garbled speech in cubicle 3" becomes a person again, an eloquent, Armani-dressed trial lawyer, who just yesterday won his case but now needs your help if he is ever to speak again. Stories can grab your attention and, at times, your heart. What the arts and humanities bring to medicine is the ability to recognize other people's stories as our own. This is the first step toward caring.

Stories have other powers, including the power to deceive. The ability to examine stories critically is a vital tool for any population that is to remain free and democratic. The study of theatre, art, music, philosophy, literature, and all the humanities gives us this training while at the same time teaching us that learning about other people's stories can help us, as global citizens, foster mutual understanding and tolerance.

The arts and the humanities are stories waiting to be understood and from that understanding influence who we are and what we can become. Give us our stories, and teach us how to reflect upon them. What could be more useful?

In many cultures the old tell stories: it's called wisdom.

Regarding African Modernist Art

Salah Hassan

Africa is a complex intellectual construct that means different things to different people. But, for sure, Africa is also a diverse and highly complex historical entity. For the last four centuries, due to experiences of slavery, colonialism, and the resultant mass displacement and diaspora of African peoples and cultures, it is no longer possible to speak of Africa or African as a mere geographic entity. Whatever it is we mean by "African," including of course African modernism, is the product of this historically complex entity and global presence. The question still remains: what is African modernism?

Modern art practice, in European or other contexts, signals a sense of difference, a self-conscious process of refashioning the self and the projection of particular attitudes towards the past and the present. This is what makes it hard to have a fixed definition of modernity, as it is by nature fluid and constantly subject to renewal. Hence, the claim to modernity, as once suggested by Rasheed Araeen among others, is wide open and not necessarily a universalized European construct or monopoly.

Two points must be emphasized in relation to modernity or modernism in general: the plurality of modernity, even in its

European context, and the realization that there are other modernisms beyond the European context. As Paul Wood argued in *The Challenge of the Avant-Garde* (1999), we can "look at some ways in which the concept has been used and try to draw out some of the central preoccupations of the modernists." Modernity, as defined by many scholars today, engages those social changes implied in becoming modern, i.e., urbanization, industrialization, wage labor and factory systems, etc. Modernism designates artistic practices associated with modernity.

For the purposes of visual art, modernity has been understood as a major transformative social force by the mid nineteenth century. The theories of Baudelaire on transient beauty, shock, and fleeting and ephemeral experiences of urban life become widely influential, especially through their interpretation by Walter Benjamin. Marx emphasizes the centrality of capitalist exchange and commodification as the main feature of modern life. Max Weber suggested that social life under modernity is characterized by bureaucratization, rationalization, and secularization. T.J. Clark, in his recent book *Farewell to an Idea*, reaffirms this understanding of modernity, which refers to the great social transformation associated with modern life.

On the other hand, "modernism" specifically refers to the aesthetic, artistic, and representational practices associated with modernity. A narrower, privileged sense of modernism refers to the great period of European and American artistic experimentation between 1880–1940. Not all art produced under "modernity" is considered "modernist"; the latter term is generally reserved for the avant-garde art of its time.

Avant-garde, an essential concept to modernist practice, continues to designate the most adventurous and experimental forms of art practice during the nineteenth and twentieth centuries, and also indicates a relationship of art with politics. Inevitably, the characterization of the avant-garde excludes the majority of work produced during any specific period.[1]

This "official history" of Western modernism leaves out the massive infusions of non-Western artists and cultures. Non-Western artists based in the West have not received the critical recognition they deserve, and they remained sidelined in art historical texts on twentieth century art.

Exclusionary mechanisms are built into the very definition of the dominant narratives of modernism. As Edward Said argued in *Culture and Imperialism*, an exploration of the twentieth century history and sociology of the Western metropolis reveals the strong presence of students, writers, and artists from previously colonized territories, including Africa, in European capitals. Said also pointed out that their intellectual production is essential to any reconsideration of global modernity as it overlaps with their contemporary European counterparts, and their intellectual and cultural production can in no way be analyzed as merely reactive assertions of separate native or colonized subjectivity.

The exclusionary mechanisms built into the definitions of modernity, modernism, and the avant-garde have attracted a number of important critiques from within Europe and from non-Western perspectives. "Modernism" is seen as an ideological operation that prevents other understandings of modern life through realist narrative and symbolic modes, which were excluded by emphasis only on experimental and alienated modernist avant-gardes.[2]

Said further points out that it has taken a long time and a remarkable adjustment in perspective and understanding "to take account of the contribution to modernism of decolonization resistance culture, and the literature of opposition to imperialism."

What Foucault once called "subjugated knowledges" have exploded in the form of first-class literature and scholarship by postcolonial intellectuals who challenge the canons of domains once controlled by a Western Judeo-Christian tradition. Paris, London or Rome provide examples of how African and Caribbean immigrant writers, poets, and artists have laid claim to the space of the Western metropolis and reworked ideas of exile, nation, and citizenship in ways that defy easy readings of "otherness." One example is *Presence Africaine*, the Congress of Pan African intellectuals of 1954 in Paris and 1956 in Rome.

According to Dipesh Chakrabarty, the disciplinary practice of writing history unwittingly produces a singular, universal history formatted to the template provided by the history of the West. As a result, "the non-West must play the role of the outside, the otherness that creates the boundary of the space of modernity," as suggested by Timothy Mitchell.

In this view, modernity of the margins, through repetitions produced by successive acts of translation, paradoxically stabilizes the idea of the modern yet simultaneously undermines it.

A contrasting and possibly more hopeful view is provided by Stuart Hall:

"The world is moving outwards and can no longer be structured in terms of the centre/periphery relation. It has to be defined in terms of a set of interesting centres, which are both different from and related to one another. If you think about where important movements are being made, sometimes they happen in the centre, but the most exciting artists are those who live simultaneously in the centre and at the periphery. We are embarking on a hundred different ideas of "the modern," not one, and therefore of a thousand practicing modern artists ..."

Said, Chakraparty, Mitchell, and Hall, among others, are helpful in our effort to define and theorize African modernity and reposition African modernism vis-à-vis the discourse of global modernism. They also provide a glimpse of the difficulties of theorizing modernity and modernism outside the West.

The following characteristics are associated with the origin and development African modernism:
• By European standards, the period we designate as modern in Africa is certainly short, and modernism in African terms is certainly much more recent — as the title of Okwui Enwezor's landmark exhibition, *The Short Century*, has implied and as

the period of 1945–1994, on which he chose to focus, clearly indicates. However, modernism is uneven as a phenomenon within the African continent. In Egypt and other parts of North Africa one could trace instances of modernity as early as the turn of the twentieth century.

• African modernism is also marked by slavery, colonialism, and the violent rupture it created with tradition. The conscious claim to modernity implies a sense of resistance, for modernity in Africa was borne out of the struggle for decolonization. Integral to this moment is the rise of national consciousness and the modernist project of nation building. In this context one should critically approach the roles played by European and Western patronage and intervention, European expatriates, colonial administrators, liberal colonial educators, and missionaries who have contributed to the rise of the modern art movements in Africa.

• The most important factor in the rise of African modernism has been the nationalistic cultural resurgence that swept many newly independent African countries where government patronage and interest in the arts became part of nation building and refashioning of the self in modern terms. The net result has been the creation of new movements in all facets of the arts and in social life, in an attempt to construct new tropes of self-representation. In that sense, one could argue that African modernity is nationalist. However, the nature of the political ideologies, programs, and strategies adopted by leaders and movements of independence and liberation in Africa was also internationalist.

• As documented in the literature in fields other than the visual arts, the African modernist project has existed in the intersections of Pan-Africanism and Pan-Arabism, the struggle for liberation and decolonization, and the intellectual dialectics this struggle symbolizes in the relationships among Africa, the West, and the world. The Algerian war for liberation, the anti-Apartheid movement, and the Palestinian struggle for self-determination — all are closely scrutinized in literature and documented through photography and film.

Several exhibitions and a few texts produced during the last decade have captured aspects of the complexity of African modernity effectively through interdisciplinary and visual culture approaches. These include exhibitions such as *Seven Stories about Modern Art in Africa*, *The Short Century*, *Authentic/Ex-Centric*, *Looking Both Ways*, *A Fiction of Authenticity*, and *Africa Remix*. With varying degrees of success, these exhibitions provided critical frameworks for interrogating African modernism and postmodernism by engaging media including art, cloth, posters, photography, architecture, music, theater, fashion, film, and literature.

These exhibitions have directly or indirectly transcended the typical representation of Africa prevalent in the discipline. They broke down the artificial boundaries between North and Sub-Saharan Africa, so-called Arab Africa and Black Africa, and stood in clear contrast to essentializing tendencies, which plague the field of African art and presentation or representation in texts.

The general state of research on contemporary and modern African has improved a great deal in the last two decades, and a number of well-researched books, dissertations, and exhibitions and companion catalogues have been produced.

Contemporary African artists in the international arena have started to enjoy some recognition.

Few books written in the last three decades have focused on documenting African artists of the caliber of Ernest Mancoba, Ibrahim El Salahi, Skunder Boghossian, Gerard Sokoto, or have taken a critical look at their career and art works. All Western museums with an interest in African art have shied away from retrospective exhibitions dedicated to the work of a single pioneer modern African artist. The preference has so far been for thematic and group exhibitions, in which it is impossible to pay critical attention to the life and works of individual artists in a critical manner equal to their Western counterparts.

The life stories of above-mentioned African masters of modernism are a case in point. They were a key part of the story of those African and non-Western immigrants in the Western metropolises who attempted to challenge the narrative of Western modernism and to reconstruct the idea of modern art. Their work and life stories, which are central to theorizing African modernity, are part of the complex narrative of African modernism, which we must now attempt to reconstruct, theorize, and document in art historical studies as integral to the canon of modern art. The fear is that the destiny of these modern artists will become like that of the creators of those classical masterpieces, anonymous and forgotten.

[1] Paul Wood, "Introduction" in *The Challenge of the Avant-Garde* (New Haven: Yale, 1999).

[2] Raymond Williams, "When Was Modernism?" in *Art in Modern Culture: An Anthology of Critical Texts*. Edited by Francis Frascina and Jonathan Harris (London: Phaidon, 1992), 23–27.

For the Love of Books

Peter Uwe Hohendahl

It is difficult to write about the humanities without thinking about libraries, since they are the archive of the accumulated humanistic knowledge. Without any doubt the quality of libraries is essential for the work of humanists. The very idea of a literary or philosophical tradition is difficult to conceive without the material existence of books and libraries. Naturally, therefore, humanists flock to great libraries; they are their Mecca where they can be in touch with the books, prints, maps, and music sheets on which their work is based. This "being in touch" can be taken literally, for there is a strong sensual component in the use of libraries and their materials. Working in the rare-book room, walking through the stacks, or holding a specific edition of *Moby Dick* in one's hand illustrates the practices of our work. We rarely think about it because we take it for granted. When I decided to stay in the United States after a year as a postdoctoral fellow and therefore applied for positions in this country, I gave a number of plausible reasons to my family and friends but there was one that I never mentioned and possibly did not fully realize myself: the American research library and Widener Library in particular. Widener had made a deep and lasting impression on me. It was the place where I wanted to study and work. The young scholar was overwhelmed not only by the extraordinary number of books collected in Widener but also the fact that they were systematically organized and accessible to the user. This order encouraged me to browse, especially in areas outside my own discipline. I could take the books out of the stacks, read chapters, examine the index, find links to other books that stood right next to them. What makes the use of American research libraries so exciting is the physical organization of the books on the shelves; the arrangement reflects the order of the intellectual world that they represent. When a book has been given a call number in the Library of Congress system, it has become part of that order.

Libraries as we know them were built for collecting books and other printed materials — that is to say they are part of the Gutenberg era. But how far will this era extend into the future? And how will the rise of the electronic media impact the status of the physical object called "book"? It is becoming increasingly apparent that the new media will also redefine the world of publishing and thereby the fate of the book. However, to what extent this development will transform the working conditions and practices of the humanities is not yet clear. But it is unlikely that we will simply lose the book, that digital records will systematically replace the vast holdings of print materials in libraries. The use of books, especially those that contain important cultural texts, cannot be reduced to the storage of information. As physical objects they influence our use; the typeset, the paper, the binding, and the cover — these make a difference. They speak to us through our senses and define the aura of a book, the way it becomes unique in our use of a particular copy. Like living beings, books age and show the signs of this process, either as mere deterioration or as an increase of their auratic power. Yet even a copy of Nietzsche's *Zarathustra* that is falling apart after many years of use possibly remains special to its owner who has intensively worked on this text. Underlining and notes in the margins testify to this process. The use makes books very personal objects whose value cannot be measured in monetary terms. When a colleague of mine recently lost a substantial part of his library by flooding, he mourned above all the loss of his marks and annotations in the damaged books, in short, precisely the signs of intensive use that would decrease the exchange value of the books in the eyes of a book dealer. He could replace many of the books but not the physical expression of his intellectual labor.

Why do humanists collect books in the first place? Would it not suffice to use the copies stored in the library? Ostensibly, humanists collect books for professional reasons. One's personal library guarantees uninterrupted access to the texts that one needs either for teaching or research. But this pragmatic argument is in many cases a cover for other and sometimes less rational reasons. Collecting books and building a personal library are motivated by desires that are only partially or not at all related to professional needs. It is a creative act, namely the attempt to generate a spiritual world or, to be more precise, the material representation of a spiritual world. But, as we know from famous private collections, the books brought together will not necessarily be read. For the owner it may suffice that they stand together on a shelf, physical evidence of a spiritual realm, even if no one fully explores this realm. Above all, collecting books and building a personal library is an adventure that consumes time and energy, not to mention financial resources. This is the reason why second-hand bookstores and catalogues are so much more exciting than books in print found in regular bookstores. There is the search for a specific edition that can take years, but also the unexpected discovery of a book unrelated to one's research interests that one picks up out of curiosity.

Can we make the argument that humanists are more likely to collect books and build private libraries? I am not certain that a systematic argument can be offered, but it seems to me that humanists have a different relationship to books than natural and social scientists. In those disciplines the concept of scientific progress, according to which only the most recent publications are relevant, defines the use of books and articles. Older materials become the objects of the history of science. In the humanities this notion of linear progress is not compelling, since it is the cultural tradition itself that defines the parameters of humanistic work. Furthermore, although the interpretation of this tradition is constantly in flux, the quality of this work cannot be assessed in terms of abstract improvement over time. Therefore the return to an older book or essay may be more helpful than the fixation on the latest publication.

One of the requirements of scholarly work in the humanities is the use of critical editions, which offer a text of the poem or novel that is as close as possible to the author's intentions.

We all are familiar with those comprehensive editions on which generations of philologists have worked. But do we always use them when we read a favorite work or author? I must confess that I occasionally prefer to go back to editions to which I am personally attached, books that I bought as a student or that I received as a gift from friends. Reading the novels of Theodor Fontane, for instance, a representative of realism in German literature, I was deeply influenced by a one-volume leather-bound edition that I found in a second-hand bookstore in Berlin in the 1950s. It was this book that awakened my interest in Fontane. Although today I own a much better critical edition, I still mourn the loss of my previous edition, which mysteriously disappeared when my library was shipped to America. Similarly, I still prefer the early editions of Walter Benjamin's work published by Suhrkamp to the more recent critical edition, since these heavily marked copies are part of my own long and changing involvement with this critic. In these early editions Benjamin's world and my own intellectual interests became fused. It has been a process of appreciation that began with the acquisition of the individual book as a material object. Books standing on the shelves of a private collection thus contain not only the published texts but also the memory of reading and understanding these texts. Yet these memories are personal and cannot be transferred to another user of the same books. At best he or she can attempt to make sense of my annotations and markings.

Books on the shelves touch each other. But does their physical arrangement as a row reflect an order, a way of bringing texts together that belong together? Large research libraries impose such an order on their holdings according to a complex system. But private collections rarely care for a systematic organization. The initial phase of a private collection demands no more than a simple division, for example that between literary and scholarly works. Later when the collection has grown and expanded in space, it has developed its own organization. More divisions would be necessary, but the books seem to resist a thematic or systematic regrouping. Once they have found their place next to each other, they want to stay there. Although I have known for years that I should reorganize my own library to improve the effectiveness of the entire collection and the ease of access to individual books, I have never done it and have relied instead on my memory to find the book I need, which can be time-consuming because a book can be hidden in a number of places. The more my collection has grown in different directions, the more I have to struggle with the fact that the library has its own life and exists beyond my control. However, this recognition has not stopped me from acquiring additional books, since that decision would entail the admission that my intellectual curiosity has come to an end.

Humanities — With or Without Humanism?

Biodun Jeyifo

As one who is from the developing world and has researched, taught, and lectured on the humanities in many parts of the world, I have for a long time reflected deeply on the relationship between what is known as "theoretical antihumanism" and the humanities. This is partly because for almost all my adult, professional life, theoretical antihumanism has greatly intrigued and fascinated me. But there is also the fact that I believe that a scholar from the developing world who teaches courses in the humanities at a place like Cornell cannot afford not to take theoretical antihumanism seriously. In this short essay, I wish to explore why the convergence of these two factors — a decades-old interest in theoretical antihumanism and the enormously congenial intellectual environment for it at Cornell — have shaped the teaching, research, and mentoring agendas I have set for myself in my time at Cornell. I will also try to indicate the high stakes involved in this seemingly abstract issue. This necessarily entails a discrete foray into aspects of a personal and generational intellectual biography.

It is an important aspect of the intellectual history of the last half-century that the Althusserian and other varieties of Marxism that had become influential intellectual currents in the teaching of humanities disciplines in my graduate school days in this country in the early 1970s were strongly "antihumanist." As I had come from an intellectual background that comprised a deep and enthusiastic engagement with Sartrean and other "humanist" varieties of Western Marxism as well as the intellectual projects of the national liberation movements of the developing world, it was a daunting task for me to productively engage Althusserianism. In existentialist Sartrean Marxism and the ideas of the great theorists of Third World national liberation movements like Frantz Fanon, Jose Mariategui, and Amilcar Cabral, activists and revolutionaries were deemed to be solidly self-present in their acts and projects. This was due to the fact that for those whose societies had been oppressed by centuries of capitalism, slavery, and colonialism and their effects and legacies, human freedom and responsibility were real and measurable; they were complex indicators of collective and individual self-fashioning and self-worth. For Althusserians, the "selves" engaged in such acts and projects were "elements" in a nonhuman "structure." Moreover, if, indubitably, there was a discernible "totality" in the conditions and relations that produced these "elements," there was nonetheless no "totalizer" in the driver's seat of history or consciousness. Althusserianism was thus a hard nut to crack and a bracing system of thought to integrate with the likes of Fanon, Mariategui, Cabral, and Sartre, including the Sartre of *A Critique of Dialectical Reason*. For this reason, it helped that Althusser had made a distinction between a "humanist," in his opinion "soft" Marxism, and a "structuralist," "hard" and "scientific" Marxism. This is because in making that distinction, he tacitly acknowledged the continuing strong, if in his opinion wrong-headed, appeal of the "humanist" Marx to many activists. At any rate, it helped a lot that one had the option to tease out the tangled connections between the "humanist" and "antihumanist" currents of critical thought. For me and members of my generation who intellectually and politically came of age in the first two decades of the post-independence era in Africa, Asia, and the Caribbean, we found great ideological comfort in the availability of this option.

In the "Age of Theory," that option increasingly became unavailable as the "subject" became completely decentered as the foundation of consciousness and theoretical antihumanism became more entrenched as the "common sense" of postmodern critical thought. Indeed, it was symptomatic of this development that the "individual," "person," or "man" who had been the center of all varieties of traditional humanism metamorphosed into a "subject" who is nothing more or less than the "effect" of language, discourse, or textuality. But with the thoroughgoing deconstruction of every known anchor or "foundation" of that "subject" — God, History, Revolution, Race, Nation, Class, Gender, Tribe and, above all, Reason — theoretical antihumanism reached its apogee. This radically uncompromising antifoundationalism that provides the fundamental theoretical underpinning of antihumanism is an endlessly fascinating and, in certain respects, intellectually and politically productive rubric for engaging many of the problems associated with diverse forms of entrenched, reactionary power and authority, whether such forms of power and authority operate at global or institutional levels or at the level of personal, everyday relationships. But for Third World and minority intellectuals who, on account of the sorts of historical and political factors I have identified earlier in this essay, cannot afford not to keep the perspectives and values of humanism in sight and available, this creates a great dilemma. This dilemma arises from the fact that in totally evacuating self, identity, and experience of any anchor in positive or grounded conceptions, theoretical antihumanism seems to leave one little room for maneuver in matters of political and cultural activism. In my experience at Cornell, I have discovered that this dilemma finds a resolution in the question that stands at the title of this essay, the question of whether or not the humanities — fiction, poetry, drama, film, dance; the plastic, visual, and digital arts; and the educational curricula that consolidate and expand their production, reception, and vitality — can be deemed to be with or without "humanism." In my 17 years at Cornell, it has been my experience that this question has not been as abstract or factitious as it may seem. Permit me to use a brief elaboration of this observation to bring this essay to a conclusion.

Not as a set of postulates or an elaborated system of ideas but as a style of thought and an idiom of discourse, theoretical antihumanism has been the sustaining intellectual motive force for the work of many colleagues of distinction and also of many graduate students of exceptional intellectual promise. This has been the defining reality against which to take a measure of the enormously significant fact that while in the same period at Cornell there has been an unceasing struggle to keep the humanities vibrant, supported, and competitive, that struggle has never, to the best of my knowledge, been organized under the banner and the sign of theoretical antihumanism. If irrefutable, factual evidence can be produced to disprove this contention, I will accept such evidence because intellectual integrity demands no less. But I would accept such evidence also because it can in no way invalidate my suspicion that the humanities are best defended and consolidated by a combination of robustly humanist and cannily antihumanist traditions of critical thought. For even if I have not personally encountered a defense of the humanities made in the name of theoretical antihumanism, it is conceivable to think of aspects of a humanities program that is founded on antihumanist traditions of critical thought and the particular values of radical, uncompromising skepticism that they embody. One thinks here of the mainstream of modernist and postmodernist art and much of the experimental work of all ages. That said, it remains true and indubitable that humanism remains the basic theoretical bedrock of the humanities. What remains to be said is that one talks here of a "humanism" that cannot afford to place theoretical antihumanism out of sight in a zone of oblivion.

Poetry and the Common Sense

Rayna Kalas

Does the study of literature have to be useful? Since many people consider the study of literature to be, at best, a luxury, and, at worst, a soft cover for the peddling of ideology, it is a question that should be asked. Some will answer "no" on the grounds that literature is about pleasure, not utility (and their detractors will call them profligate or decadent). And some will answer "yes" on the grounds that all literature is social praxis (and their detractors will call them propagandists or didacts). Neither answer offers a particularly satisfying (or foolproof) way for thinking about why the study of literature might be a social value. But one can see how responses would polarize in this way as long as utility serves as the principal category of judgment. An elaborated explanation of how figurative language continually transposes social and intellectual realities would give us a better sense of the social importance of the study of literature, and yet the imperative to think of literature as a utility, as the instrumental means toward a more privileged end, seems to inhibit disclosures of that kind.

Allegations about literary study being too worldly, or not worldly enough, come from outside the university, but the same basic argument is waged within academic circles. Among English faculty, there are those who caution that our approaches to literature, and even the category of literature itself, are not neutral but are predicated upon social, cultural, and aesthetic hierarchies whose exclusions should at the very least be exposed, if not corrected, within our field of study. On the other side, there are those who worry that, by expanding the objects of our study to virtually any aspect of culture, literary critics may be forfeiting our stewardship of a discipline that engenders its unique form of knowledge and practice not simply through its mastery of the arts of rhetoric but also through its understanding of figurative language. Should our goal, as teachers and researchers, be to democratize our own intellectual practice and to make any aspect of culture available for any person's analysis, even if it means that what we would then hold in common is a notion of "reading" that is synonymous with critique? Should our goal instead be to preserve our guardianship over a more rarefied form of "reading," even if it means that, in doing so, we perpetuate the nostalgia for a unity of intellectual values that never really existed?

What these questions are really agonizing over — the relationship between social privileges and private ideals, and between common sense and uncommon understanding — is as old as humanism itself. By way of illustration, but also as a reminder that humanism is almost never as tidy or triumphant as later categorizations of it have suggested, I offer a passage from Ralph Robynson's 1556 English translation of Thomas More's *Utopia*. The passage is taken from the very last paragraph of the book, where the character, More, having listened to Raphael Hythloday's account of Utopian society, demurs that the "manner and laws of that people seemed to be instituted and founded of no good reason." The one thing that "More" just cannot let go of, the one bit of common sense that he just cannot shake, is his belief in private property, and the passage gently mocks him for it. He finds fault with the Utopians *"chiefly, in … the principal foundation of all their ordinances, that is to say in the community of their life and living, without any occupying of money* by which thing only all nobility, magnificence, worship, honor, and majesty, *the true ornaments and honors, as the common opinion is, of a commonwealth, utterly be overthrown and destroyed"* [emphasis added].[1] The implication here is that "More" just does not get it. As for Raphael, he too is guilty of obduracy. And in the end, very little seems resolved. *Utopia* establishes an impasse between the "occupying of money" and a "community of life and living," between common sense and uncommon experience and between true wisdom and wise praxis. Yet what makes the book so interesting and so troubling is that these oppositions rarely line up in any predictable way or along any single axis. I suspect that More, the author, was making fun of a contradiction that lies at the very heart of humanism: its vaunted purpose of serving both the private interest and the public good.

By the time More was writing, Italian humanism had fallen into, as Jacob Burckhardt puts it, "a deep and general disgrace" brought about by "unbridled subjectivity."[2] It is true that the advent of printing played its part: since the dissemination of the printed text obviated the need for "personal intercourse with the humanists," scholars were no longer "personally the possessors and diffusers of ancient culture." But the humanists themselves were principally to blame. "Of all men who ever formed a class, they had the least sense of their common interest, and least respected what there was of this sense."[3] Humanism survived, I would argue, in two strains that grew increasingly distinct: humanism as an educational practice and humanism as a form of poetic erudition. When we speak of humanism today, we are principally speaking about the legacy of the former — about an institutionalized rhetoric rather than the playfully irreverent figurative language of writers like Rabelais, Erasmus, and More. Those writers were satirizing some of humanism's rationalism and "unbridled subjectivity" — its exclusivity, its rhetoric of political and diplomatic efficacy, and its propensity toward self-entitlement — in order to preserve some of its more imaginative and collective forms. *Utopia*, originally printed, as it was written, in a punning, erudite form of Latin prose, preserves an elite language of learning, even as it engaged in the dispersal of that discourse. The text presents a conversational exchange among a group of humanists who were Thomas More's actual contemporaries and yet included among their number a fictional character, Raphael Hythloday. Though his last name essentially means "distributor of nonsense," it is Raphael who offers the most incisive critique of English society.

Utopia satirizes both the players and the principles of humanism. With its dual purpose of serving both private interests and the public concern, humanistic reason will always be circumscribed by the social organization. The result, as *Utopia* so scathingly points out, is that wisdom itself has taken the shape of private ownership. "More's" very notion of what is "true" observes the social logic of property. He withholds his disagreements, he admits, because Raphael "had reprehended this fault in other, which be afeard lest they should seem not to be wise enough unless they could find fault in other men's inventions." Wisdom is, for More, an "ornament and honor," he cannot conceive of it apart from private property. Of course, Raphael himself finds fault with fault-finders; even in positioning himself against the private ownership of property, he is circumscribed by its logic. Raphael and the character More both have critiques, Raphael of English society, "More" of Utopian society; they both find fault, assert wisdom. The book even solicits the fault-finding and proprietary wisdom of an uncommon reader by placing "More" and Raphael, England and Utopia, side by side, and by making them so available for comparison and judgment.

Humanistic reason may urge its subjects to compare and judge, but humanistic reading seems to engender another kind of understanding entirely. It is the figurative language of this work — etymological puns, quibbles, riddles, repetitions — that makes it possible to learn and observe the relationship between wisdom and property without picking sides, assuming a position, or asserting, as a reader-critic, the proprietary identity of a fixed opinion. It is figurative language in this work that makes possible, not unbridled assertions of wisdom, but understanding. Figurative language, we might say, creates a common understanding out of uncommon sense. No matter how clever the reader, understanding stems not from reason or opinion but from the commonly held medium of language.

There are all kinds of issues, inside and outside of the classroom, on which a faculty member or a student, like any citizen, must take a clear and unequivocal stand. But I do not think the argument needs to be made that the humanities disciplines have been essential in providing us with the rhetorical, oratorical, and logic skills that are necessary to take positions in that way; our culture on the whole accepts that as a given. The strain of humanism that saw itself principally as an educational practice for the fashioning of gentleman subjects has enjoyed a rather vigorous and enduring (and sometimes vicious and exclusionary) legacy within the institution of the university and indeed within the culture at large. What does, I think, need to be acknowledged is that we have, by and large, forfeited the legacy of a different strain of early humanism, a strain of humanism that understood figurative language as a collective form of understanding and a social good. What we might carry away from that strain of humanism is the recognition that figurative language engages our interests as members of a collectivity and as speakers of a language, rather than as masterful agents of subjective reason; and it does so by cyclically troping or transposing proper pleasure and common benefit. What the humanistic disciplines let go of in losing sight of that strain of humanism was the potential to make it our very basic premise that figurative language actually does things in the world.

Humanism set up from the outset an agon between intellectual distinction and social concern, between private interests and the common weal. The only thing more futile than trying to resolve an impasse that is endemic to the whole history of humanism would be trying to do so without realizing that the legacy of humanism has in fact already been spent. I do not mean by this that the humanities are doomed, only that humanism, if it even still is one of the defining features of our culture at large (plenty of people would say that we are already "posthumanist"), will not be so for long. To my thinking it is the phrase "ownership society" that rings the death knell of humanism. An ownership society is the necessary outcome of humanism and its undoing: it fulfils the educational agenda of humanism as a means of entitlement, but it overrides the poetic agenda of humanism as an expression of collective intelligence; it resolves the struggle between private interests and the common weal into a system in which private interests are the only social good. English departments will have much more to lose if we think of ourselves only as conservators of culture and purveyors of wisdom. But English departments stand to gain both purpose and resolve if we recognize that voice and figure in language are reality-based expressions of collective interest that cannot be measured or codified as property or utility.

[1] Sir Thomas More, *Utopia*, trans. Ralph Robynson [1556], ed. David Harris Sachs (Boston and New York: Bendford/St. Martin's, 1999), 201.

[2] Jacob Burckhardt, *The Civilization of the Renaissance in Italy*, trans., S.G.C. Middlemore (New York: Penguin Books, 1990), 177.

[3] Burckhardt, 177 and 179.

What Is Essential to the Humanities?

Dominick LaCapra

Are the humanities useful? What is essential to them? Is their usefulness what defines what they essentially are or should be?

At least in the general public, the question of usefulness would in all probability seldom arise with respect to the natural or even the social sciences. The question might rather be how one could avert certain dangerous uses or abuses of them (the making of so-called weapons of mass destruction or the development of techniques of total surveillance and control). That the question of usefulness is so readily and prevalently posed about the humanities might be interpreted as symptomatic of a defensive posture as well as of a feeling that the humanities are essentially of no real use, whether positive or negative. The response to this orientation seems relatively obvious: the humanities may not essentially be of short-term use or deliver immediate, technological pay-offs (although literature or philosophy majors may, of course, find jobs in communications or go to law school). The "use" of the humanities is more indirect and long-term. As is often said, they contribute to the quality of life, and the fact that people in retirement return to the study of humanistic subjects is testimony simultaneously to their centrality and to their marginality in our culture. I would in any case suggest that their pursuit is more than a sign of their function as status symbols or "cultural capital." It is also an indication of their valorization as components of worthwhile experience and a life that is more than one-dimensional. Indeed the nature and role of the humanities at their best go beyond use-value (and its complement in a utilitarian, pragmatic, capitalistic frame of reference: exchange as well as money-making value). The humanities point in the direction of generosity and gift-giving. The latter provide one important meaning of "liberal" in the term "liberal arts," and the humanities are liberal arts par excellence. And while they go beyond narrowly conceived use-value or practicality, they are not entirely useless, for they create bonds, sometimes very durable bonds, and they are both good to think with and good to live with.

A spirit of liberality, generosity, and gift-giving can be proposed as essential to the humanities — essential not in some dogmatic or exclusive sense (it may in fact also characterize significant aspects of work in the sciences) but in a sense that stipulates what is important and relatively distinctive but continually open to debate and contestation. For the latter qualities may also be seen as essential to humanistic understanding and exchange, and argument or even polemic can be undertaken in a liberal, generous spirit. Indeed one might contend that an intelligent, informed, spirited critique is a better gift than a conventional, vapid encomium. Moreover, inquiry into a problem cannot be a zero-sum game or competition since the recurrently debatable question is the nature and relative value of contributions to problems that do not lend themselves to a definitive solution or first-time discovery. Basic problems in the humanities are repeated (and repeatedly thought about) with variations over time, and temporality itself from a humanistic perspective is this very process of repetition with variation or change, occasionally abrupt, decisive, or even traumatic change. (However it is construed or misconstrued, "modernity" is often seen as marking one such traumatic break or "shock" experience.)

Here a crucial distinction is that between problems and puzzles. A puzzle (or puzzle-like "problem") may be solved, and its solution has an immediate use-value (how does one build a more efficient engine or devise a faster way of accessing the Internet?). Puzzles have a place in all studies, including the humanities (for example, the dating of a document, the attribution of a text, or the identification of a reference or allusion). As important, even more important, are problems into which one inquires and which one may elucidate or even deepen but not solve. If asked to propose a single sentence to designate what is essential to the humanities, I would offer the following: the study of cross-disciplinary problems that are not narrowly utilitarian but instead allow one to intervene in, or contribute to, an open, questioning, and self-questioning process of inquiry as well as implicate the self in relation to those processes and to the past itself in ways that may enable possible, and possibly more desirable, futures. How should one understand the terms of this "definition" of what is essential as well as liberally empowering in the humanities?

Cross-disciplinary is not simply interdisciplinary in that it does not merely combine existing disciplines to investigate and provide better answers to existing questions. It inquires into problems that themselves cut across existing disciplines, may be treated with different emphases or inflections in them, and perhaps even suggest the need for newer disciplines, subdisciplines, or institutional units such as programs and departments. What are some cross-displinary problems that may be elucidated but not solved as if they were puzzles? Without pretending to be all-inclusive and exhaustive, one might mention violence, victimization, surviving, mourning, trauma, and oppression but also gift-giving, trust, compassion, responsibility, agency, community- and institution-building, laughter, and joy, as well as the sacred and sacrifice. Sacrifice is particularly knotty from an ethical and political perspective since it typically conflates oblation (or gift-giving) and victimization, with the victim as the gift to a higher being or even as an offering when there is no belief in a determinate higher being or personalized deity. And sacrifice may be displaced into secular contexts in often obscure and disavowed ways, appearing in the form of a cult of violence or a belief that through violence (even victimization) one may regenerate or redeem the self or the group.

How could one possibly solve such problems and processes as trauma, victimization, sacralization, sacrifice, trusting, assuming or ascribing responsibility, and gift-giving? One can at best work on and through them in a manner that more or less "usefully" expands the possibility of accentuating whatever may be judged to be desirable in them and opposing, diminishing, or even eliminating what is judged to be undesirable. Hence, with respect to sacrifice, the challenge (should one call it humanistic or posthumanistic since it concerns not only humans but also other animals?) is to valorize the gift while disengaging it from, and counteracting, victimization.

A recent cross-disciplinary problem that has risen to prominence, notably in its relation to extreme events (such as rape, abuse, and genocide), is trauma, and trauma theory or trauma studies not only crosses disciplinary boundaries within the humanities but even involves the sciences and social sciences (neurophysiology, social psychology, psychoanalysis, psychiatry, narrative medicine). One might argue that, like trauma, the most essential problems in the humanities are precisely those that are not "owned" by any given humanistic discipline but often studied, at times with unsettling or uncanny effects, in various disciplines, including disciplines not generally seen as humanistic. They are also the problems that are not confined to the academy but have a bearing on the public sphere and the larger society.

A similar point might be made about specific texts, art works, artifacts, and, more recently, media that are studied in the humanities. What discipline "owns" the works of Sophocles, Dante, Freud, Virginia Woolf, Fellini, or Picasso? One or another may be studied more in one discipline than in another. But would a scholar in art history or visual studies be justified in prohibiting a discussion of Picasso in literature or history? What is distinctive about basic humanistic works or texts is the way their significance exceeds any given discipline. And they may be appreciated, read, or studied outside the academy. Indeed the degree to which they enter the public sphere is an index of general culture, including the richness and diversity of a culture that combines such interests with prevalent forms of popular and media culture. Popular media themselves are enlivened, enhanced, and at times critically challenged by a sustained relation to so-called high or elite culture — and vice versa. Just as Walter Benjamin would not be Walter Benjamin without both an intimate knowledge of traditional high culture and arresting insights into popular culture, so Monty Python or the Beatles would not be what they are without a comparable interaction between the high and low or elite and popular. (No song is more "Heideggerian," indeed a tribute to Gelassenheit, than "Let It Be"!) Both elite and popular culture tend to become involuted, mannered, and even mindless to the extent their range of reference and concern remains insular. And a prominent feature of high cultures not only in modernity or postmodernity but across the ages has been (with rare exceptions) their sustained interaction with popular cultures, including the popular carnivalesque culture of laughter. The difficulty in this respect is not the existence of "canons." The latter exist even in popular culture. The unfortunate possibility is insularity as well as the process of canonization when a canon is used for exclusionary and discriminatory social and political purposes.

A criterion of a humanistic approach is a certain relation to its past, including canons as institutions which help constitute that past in changing ways. A science may rest on the belief that whatever is essential to it that comes from the past has been integrated into the present state of the art. Hence a physicist *qua* physicist may not experience a professional need to read Newton or Einstein, or a biologist to read Darwin.

These figures are studied in intellectual history or perhaps in science studies, which straddles (like much of history) the social sciences and the humanities. One might well argue that a cultured biologist should in fact read Darwin. But such a claim would relate to a broader, quasihumanistic or "liberal" understanding of what a cultured biologist as a scholar and an intellectual should be. (By the same token, a truly cultured humanist should have at least basic literacy in the sciences and social sciences.) But, without ever having read Einstein or Darwin, a scientist could well win the Nobel Prize for a contribution based on relativity or evolutionary theory. Such a state of affairs would be unacceptable, or at least raise eyebrows, only if natural sciences were to be defined in broader sociocultural and intellectual terms that would make certain "externalities" more internal to the definition of the discipline. These internalized externalities might, of course, also include the role of critical responses to forms of experimentation (notably on other animals) and to possible "uses" of discoveries.

The humanistic relation to the past assumes it is still part of the present with implications for the future. Aspects of the past, including its canonical texts or artifacts, may well be criticized but must also be known and play a key role in the present state of inquiry. For in the humanities the very way the past and its artifacts are read, reread, and responsively understood is constitutive of learning processes and renewal in the present. Moreover, the relation to the past, its processes, and its artifacts is self-implicating. The observer is implicated in the object of observation in a way that cannot be confined to one, easily bracketed dimension of research (for example, with respect to the observation of very small particles). Self-implication extends throughout the entire range of significant inquiry (and in the humanities the small, seemingly insignificant, easily bracketed detail may be the site of displacement of the most valorized, affectively charged problems). In psychoanalysis, this relation to the other is termed transference. And once it is distinguished from its more circumscribed Oedipal and familial context, transference implies that the observer or inquirer tends to displace and repeat on a basic level processes active in the other or object of research that s/he studies. Hence, for example, the student of the Holocaust confronts the transferential problem even on the elementary level of naming or terminology, for especially in emotionally charged, value-laden areas of study, there are no neutral or innocent terms. If one uses "Holocaust," one may stir the sediment of sacrificialism, for etymologically the term refers to a burnt offering. If one resorts to "final solution," one repeats Nazi terminology, and the use of scare quotes is a necessary precaution that may always be ignored or misread. "Shoah" bears witness to the role of the media in modern culture, for its use was not widespread before the appearance of Claude Lanzmann's film in the mid-1980s, and the term may have an exoticizing potential for those who do not know Hebrew. Even Nazi genocide (perhaps the most neutral of terms) still seems to grant a proprietary hold over the genocide to the Nazis and, however unintentionally or remotely, realize their desire to totally dispose of Jews (including the question of how Jews would be remembered). The point here is not to foster nominalism or engender terminological disarray but to indicate the necessity of careful qualification and the need to be sensitive to one's "transferential" implication in processes.

The broader need is to work through a relation to the past rather than blindly and even compulsively repeat its processes, at times with fatalistic, negative results. Such a caveat indicates the limitations of full objectification of the other, whereby self-implication (or transference) is disavowed or denied but typically acted out in uncontrolled, unacknowledged fashion. But it also signals the crucial importance of careful, indeed meticulous, research and close reading that may check inevitable projective and repetitive tendencies that are especially insistent to the extent a problem is still alive and pressing. The problems I have signaled in relation to the Holocaust are prevalent in history, especially in the case of extreme, traumatizing events such as genocides, and pose particularly insistent challenges not only to the humanities but to all related forms of research and understanding.

A final point about humanism and the humanities is on the cusp between critical theory and generosity or gift-giving as well as on the threshold between humanistic and other forms of understanding, including the scientific and social-scientific. And the gift in question cannot be seen as going in a one-directional sense from the human to the other. It depends on the differences within the human, especially including those brought about by being a human animal — from a certain perspective, a kind of hybrid or compromise formation. Indeed the horizon of humanism may well be posthumanistic in a specific sense. Along with such crucial questions as race, class, sexuality, and gender (all of which have been intimately bound up with issues of victimization and its relation to survivorship and agency), one should also stress the role of species, which may well be the next major concern in a critical and self-questioning humanistic approach. The concern for species gives a needed twist to the sometimes parochial, self-centered interest in the global and transnational, and it is intimately bound up with broad ecological issues. Indeed the humanities have traditionally had their covert scapegoat that global studies may itself repeat, even when the values asserted are purportedly universalistic or at least worldwide. The other-than-human animal has typically been the constitutive other of humanism and the humanities, and there has been a recurrently displaced, compulsively repeated quest to find the essential criterion (or theologian's and philosopher's stone) that decisively separates the human from other animals, in the process justifying virtually any "use" of other animals by humans. This elusive criterion, which often functions as a disavowal of the animal in the human, has taken many forms (creation in the image and likeness of God, soul, spirit, reason, freedom, language, and so forth — but not the capacity to suffer, be traumatized, be victimized, be trusting, or be joyful). What has become increasingly obvious is that the criterion can never be established with the decisiveness and, more essentially, with the invidious and exploitative consequences, with which it has been overtly or covertly postulated. And the genuine problem may lie not simply in the elusiveness of the object of the quest but in the misguided nature of undertaking the quest itself and the kinds of invidious, typically self-congratulatory investments to which it attests. This realization, which cannot be confined within the anthropocentric realm of animal "rights," should bring about an essential shift in the self-understanding of the humanities (or posthumanities) whose nature and implications are in the process of emerging. And it reopens the question of the relation between humanistic, scientific, and social-scientific disciplines. It is clearly a basis on which the humanities will have to be extensively rethought and in whose generous terms its other crucial concerns will have to be reconfigured, in certain ways from the ground up. In a word, what is essential to the humanities may now require a posthumanistic orientation that both counters the hypocrisy of a human dignity at least implicitly based on a scapegoat mechanism and generously extends the field of concern to other-than-human animals and to the differences within the human as well.

The Practical Humanities

Rose Ellen Lessy

After they earn their BAs, most of our students will spend most of their lives pursuing profit and efficiency. And in the spirit of efficiency, some of these students (or, perhaps, their parents) will worry that there is nothing to be gained from a course devoted to Norse mythology, or Taiwanese cinema, or Latin lyric poetry. And they are largely correct: there is nothing to be gained, there is no profit, and there is nothing at all efficient about the great mess that is the humanities.

Of course, some students will object to the narrow thinking of their pragmatist peers. The humanities are not useless, they will contend. Think of how impressive it will be when you can quote a relevant passage from Shakespeare at that company cocktail party. Don't forget how important effective writing skills are in the business world.

And, in large part, college English departments have accepted something of this logic: we remind the student shopping for courses that as an English major he will learn to be a good reader, a good writer, an effective communicator with strong critical thinking skills. In recent years we have been eloquent (because that is what we do best) in our endorsement of this most pragmatic defense of the humanities. We agree with the students who are concerned about the efficiency of their curricula: you can ignore the subject matter, we concede, it's the skill set that really matters. And if we are eloquent enough, we may convince them. We may in fact convince them of what they already believe to be true: that the purpose of college is to make them more profitable when they get out of college.

This is, I fear, a rather short-sighted strategy. We buy ourselves a few more English majors but at a dear price indeed: we buy them by endorsing their vision of a starkly utilitarian education, by endorsing the very logic that will eventually render us extinct.

The high-school students who now make it into elite universities and colleges have in part succeeded because they learned to manage the kinds of harrowing schedules that used to be reserved for medical residents and first-year legal associates: it is no wonder, then, that these students demand of their college curricula a certain quantifiable value. And considering the amount of debt students take on in order to attend college, we can hardly blame them for being anxious to see speedy returns on their investments. And so they shall see them. These students are already savvy workers and managers, well-trained in the not-so-fine art of multitasking; many of them require very little from us in the way of practical training. Certainly, we can help them hone particular skills. But this is not, I would suggest, the primary challenge of instructors in the humanities. Rather, it is our job to offer students something quite the opposite of practical training: we can provide them with an opportunity to slow down, unplug, and experience for however fleeting a moment the pleasure of thinking for its own sake, the pleasure of reading a challenging book that will never help them get a job and enjoying it anyway. Is this a utopian argument? Perhaps. But if there isn't place for idealistic or utopian thinking among those who study literature, art, and philosophy, then we really do have very little left to offer our students.

If higher education is to avoid bifurcating into trade schools on the one hand and wealthy finishing schools on the other, we need to develop a new set of arguments about the merits of the humanities, arguments which do not, in the end, devolve into elegant defenses of the utility of practical skills we teach on the sly. The beauty of the academic humanities is that they give students a place to explore interests, passions, tangents that are not in the least bit useful. Why, then, should we refuse this beauty? Why should we concede that the arts are only a way of dressing up pre-professional training?

I understand that not everyone can afford the luxury of what I seem to be championing — which is why those of us in the humanities must continue to apply our eloquence to issues of equality and access. We must work towards a system where both admissions and access are truly need-blind, where no student has to forgo college, or even a particular college, because the tuition is too high, or because childcare is unavailable, or because classes meet at impossible hours. But in the meantime, what is more elitist than assuming that only wealthy students should have the chance to read poetry or learn the history of modern art? What is more classist than imagining the humanities as the exclusive province of those who do not have to earn their keep?

If there seems to be a contradiction here between academic philosophy and political investments, then, pedagogically speaking, all the better. For the generative possibility of constructive contradiction is a possibility that the humanities are in a privileged position to nourish. Intellectual inquiry — like democracy itself — is not well served by streamlining. I would like to see the humanities continue as a place where students can be alive to both the thrill and the difficulty of negotiating ideas and communities that are mismatched, even incompatible. The humanities continue to be invaluable for a generation of undergraduates more focused, more driven, more professional than ever before. The humanities are invaluable not because they sharpen that focus, but because they invite another style of looking entirely.

On the Question of Value

Carolyn (Biddy) Martin

The poet, writer, artist, and scholar enrich our relation to language, enhance our ability to integrate complex thought, give us occasions for wonder, and teach us the merits of patience and concentration. Is that useful? Only if we think a supple and expressive language, human curiosity, complex thought, reverence, and communication have value.

Of what value is a poem? French writer Hélène Cixous reminds us that there is nothing more urgent than a poetic practice. "There must be a poetic practice in the political practice," an approach to the world of people and things that "leaves the other alive in her/its place." A poem teaches "the lessons of slowness," even, or especially, in times of urgency. "Caring about what seems to be of no importance, to be the insignificant, to be the well-known, the familiar, is our political urgency," writes Cixous, who urges us to not to appropriate others, not to precipitate, and not to presume. A felt sense of others and of ourselves, she reminds us, provides the grounds of ethics and respect.[1]

A fragment of Alice Fulton's poem "Garish" brings to life not only a person but the felt sense of daily-ness and the depths or surprises it can veil and disclose:

She liked white sales: the felt nap or numb
stubble of the towels, striped and creased to lush
geometries, their sensual math stacked neatly as
our taxes, which she handled with forensic ease,
or the cinderblocks, whitely amounting

to her house. She had a goodness
so decorous I'm frightened yet respectful
of the scandalous flash she chose at last.[2]

Fulton's poem gives us a feel for a woman whose chosen
end seems at odds with a certain quiet ordinariness and
decorum and yet also integral to it. Our attention is focused
on a relationship of language to its subject, of the poetic
voice to its object, and on the difficulties and wonders of one
human being's approach to another. A life and a relationship
are rendered vivid, and they open onto worlds of possible
meanings.

What then does literary criticism do? It engages our curiosity
about how things work, how a poem achieves its effects,
why it moves us, and how language incites our thoughts.
The critic extends the work of the poem by lingering over it,
calling attention to its features, analyzing its achievements,
communicating its significance. Criticism and theory also
teach Cixous's lessons of slowness and life. When M. R.
Abrams identifies in a Wordsworth poem the first use in
English literature of a particular conception of nature, he
shows that our poets and writers have made our languages
capacious enough to express what would otherwise remain
unthought. Literary critics preserve literature, thought, self-
awareness, and respect for other histories, languages, and
cultures.

We know that human beings have an extraordinary capacity to learn, yet we persist in devaluing education. It is a blessing and, in the wrong environment, perhaps something of a curse that we have such a long apprenticeship in dependence. We become who we are through the interaction of biological and social learning processes. We internalize love for those whose care we depend upon, and we are vulnerable to blind loyalty to what we believe their love and acceptance requires of us. And some loyalties can distort, even destroy our curiosity and desire to attach not only to other individuals but to entire categories of people. We also have the capacity to develop the languages and relationships that we need to reflect on what we learn and how it forms us. The humanities provide tools that every generation needs and needs throughout life.

The humanities, as a set of fields and a kind of calling, are devoted to expanding what we can experience and comprehend — what we can sense, think, understand, appreciate, express, and communicate. These are not skills that can be acquired through training. They are dimensions of character and social life that require a sensual and playful relation to language and thought. They take time, intellectual community, and awareness. They are the outcomes of an education that encourages lingering and languishing as much as it demands productivity. Their full force and free exercise require a deep engagement with language and ideas but also with oneself and with other people.

Some consider humanistic study dangerous. It has the potential to make individuals of us and to separate us from inherited ideas and limiting expectations. It also has the capacity to connect us to unapproved others by enlisting our innate curiosity about ourselves, about other people, and about the world around us. It can instill a lifelong desire for discovery, for exposure to beautiful and challenging objects, texts, and circumstances.

The study of literature was the most exhilarating experience I had in my first year at college. It also became the source of danger and, for my family, the symptom of my waywardness when I left the confines of Campbell County, Virginia, for the College of William and Mary. When I returned home from my first year away, I was greeted with dire warnings about the corrupting influence of education, of eggheads and liberals, of sissy men, horsey women, and race traitors. I was confronted with an accusation I found particularly chilling and painful. "We didn't raise you to talk like that," they said, using what seemed like exaggerations of their already very strong Southern accents. What I remember most vividly about each of my family members, ironically, is a colorful turn of phrase, a saying or an expression that defied the rote quality of the coin of the realm, which was a rhetoric of control and hate. Something in my language and speech at the end of a year in college seemed to have changed me and make me an infidel. The anti-intellectualism with which I was inundated as a child, adolescent, and young adult was aimed at ensuring loyalty to the forms of racist bigotry and social conformity that have long helped to cement familial and community bonds in that part of Virginia. Language separates even as it binds. The bonds that rely on impoverished vocabularies and thought turn out to be the most brittle and, ultimately, the most endangered by our awareness of the benefits of human diversity and inventiveness.

Reading and writing about literature allowed me to enter the world of uncontrolled ideas and to develop a different relationship not only to the world around me but also to the "I" that was struggling to find language for buried thoughts and feelings. Each significant period of growth in my life has been accompanied by the discovery or acquisition of language more adequate to the task of thinking with generosity and precision about the complexity of human experience. What captivated me about poetry and turned me into an English major was the awe it inspired when it gave expression to realms of experience that had been forbidden. It provided first a bearable and then an enjoyable solitude, and it offered hope. Hence my dismay when, in the late 1970s, at the height of feminist activism and writing, I learned again that community would always be considered by some to be defined by the limits of a common language, to borrow Adrienne Rich's words, even in groups that defined themselves in opposition to convention and constraint. The movement that had made it possible for "women to appear" (Cixous) also began to limit the forms that appearing could take. Then as now, some people on the right and the left sacrifice thought, imagination, and individuality to ideological purity. Others sacrifice these gifts to utility, defined in terms of the bottom line. Some of those people are humanists. Ultimately, however, the work of humanists is one of our most promising hedges against small-mindedness, impoverished languages, denials of history, distortions of reality, and the elevation of form over substance.

There is nothing more exhilarating or life-enhancing than to find a formulation, text, or object that transports us to other realms, that gathers our attention and focus, that makes apparent what has been obscured or left unimagined, that transforms us, and that inspires wonder. The humanities, at their best, are a celebration of transport, transformation, and wonder. The work of critique, no less than of the creative arts, enables thought, discovery, and insight by ridding us of the rigidities and exhausted forms that kill curiosity and limit us to our fears. We place enormous hope as a nation in technological innovation and the sciences that drive it, as we should. Let us put as much hope in the inventiveness of language, art, and culture, in their ability to hold open the space of the other and to make us reflect not only on our hopes but also on their limits.

Do the humanities have to be useful? Only if the human beings are intent on surviving and moving forward.

---

[1] "Poetry Is/And the Political," Hélène Cixous, from a speech delivered at the University of Wisconsin, 1980.

[2] Alice Fulton, "Garish," in the collection *Felt*, W.W. Norton, 2001, p. 44.

"everything depends on its articulation within collective assemblages of enunciation."

— Félix Guattari

Mohsen Mostafavi

One of the main topics of concern in relation to the current state of the humanities is the disjunction between what has been historically true about the humanities — namely that they are critical to human existence — and the changes in perception and opinion regarding that historic position. Contemporary humanists consider their domains of interest as relevant today as they have always been, but it is undeniable that a growing section of the populace is tending towards the evaluation of higher education primarily on the basis of purposive criteria. This tendency has created a marked divide between the humanities and the sciences, in particular; in the long run, if left unchallenged, it will not only affect the funding for the humanities (it has done so already) but could also hinder the prospect of the academy attracting a growing pool of brilliant young minds to the study of the discipline in the future.

It is an irony, therefore, that in the context of most American research universities the humanities are still generally to be found grouped in close proximity to the sciences. Often operating under the general rubric of the arts, within the Colleges of Arts and Sciences, the humanities like the sciences have become increasingly specialized. The methods of research in the humanities, however, generally differ from those in the sciences, which are invariably both collaborative and transdisciplinary. Unlike a scientist, whose laboratory is a site of speculation, detection, and documentation involving multiple agents, the humanist's reflective and synthetic task, primarily expressed through words, is a more singular and individualistic enterprise. This reality does not make one mode of practice necessarily better than the other, but it does raise the question as to whether the two can learn anything from each other. What would happen, for example, if the humanities attempted to adopt the model of research from the sciences? Would the implication of such a posture be that the humanities would de facto become more purposive and utilitarian in character? Perhaps. But that could be not just a pitfall but a potential source of innovation and discovery. The concept of collaboration across disciplines relies heavily on the balance between the achievements within a particular field and the anticipation of the benefits that arise from the close proximity as well as the hybridity of one and the other discipline.

Of course it would be incorrect to portray a situation whereby the work of humanists is carried on in isolation and that of scientists in collaboration; nevertheless it is fair to say that greater specialization in the humanities has also brought about the effect of fragmentation and isolation. This condition is partly due to the need for greater expertise for the comprehension of specialized knowledge, but it can also be attributed to the general reluctance — some might say failure — of humanists to articulate the contemporary relevance and manifestations of the humanities to a wider audience. And this points to a difficult task of negotiation — between the importance of the humanities as an endeavor that, at least in the first instance, does not have to address issues of utility and purpose, and the need for the humanities to demonstrate their purposive dimension as a precondition for engaging the other. In this context there is a good justification for the study of the humanities to involve a broad set of topics that represent, in the best sense of the word, our worldliness — that is to say, the things that matter to us and affect our very being in the world. The formation of this new type of subjectivity will in all likelihood involve some form of mediated experience. The impact on the humanities of the sciences in general and of technology in particular provides an important opportunity for the humanities and the sciences to once again consider the repercussions of their mutual interaction.

"In such conditions it appears opportune to forge a more transversalist conception of subjectivity, one which should permit us to understand both its idiosyncratic territorialized couplings (Existential Territories) and its opening onto value systems (Incorporeal Universes) with their social and cultural implications."

While paying homage to Bakhtin, Félix Guattari's reference

to a plural and polyphonic form of subjectivity enables him to recognize the "heterogeneity of the components leading to the production of subjectivity." In this way the new — transversalist — interactions between the humanities and the sciences could, for example, help address some of the problems associated with the increasing tendency to bracket off the particularities of technical change from social processes and vice versa. To achieve this type of communicative practice between the sciences and the humanities (and, by implication, a wider audience), the disciplines have to simultaneously present themselves at the level of the specific and the general, the specialist and the non-specialist. This is an important aspect of the process of participation—the reception and the ensuing capacity for the reflective remaking of the work by others. It is in this space between the work as such and its reconceptualization at a multiplicity of levels that the usefulness of the humanities will ultimately be judged. And since the humanities are still considered to be part of the arts it is imperative for the work and its production to take on the posture of artist activity. Only then will there be the possibility of seeing things in all their precariousness and uncertainties anew.

Talking Back to my Laptop:
Technology design, usefulness, and the humanities

Phoebe Sengers

So, maybe the humanities aren't so useful. Sure, they may lead to deeper philosophical understanding, help me better understand the human condition, enrich my soul — but who's got time for those things these days anyway? Rushing from meeting to meeting, squeezing in an occasional bare hour for some work that requires a modicum of thought, desperately attempting to dig out from under an ever-expanding pile of incoming email, arriving home at night so exhausted there's no option but to sack out on the sofa — I don't need more enrichment, I need to get some things done, and done fast.

Now, let's take engineering. That's useful. Give me the latest gadgets, optimize them for utility, efficiency, and productivity, and send me on my way to cut that nightmarish to-do list down to size. As a robotic vacuum cleaner winds its way around my feet, I can settle back, pull out my laptop, and batch-process tasks until the cows come home. My cell-phone-enabled PDA, my constant companion, keeps me permanently jacked in to the stream of e-mail and makes sure I remember all my deadlines and obligations. At the same time, my smart fridge takes care of my physical needs by tracking my food supply and automatically ordering more when I'm running out.

I'm lucky. Some of the best minds in our society have worked hard to make sure that I have the tools I need at my disposal to maximize my personal productivity. And, honestly, they have done an amazing job.

So it may seem a bit odd that some of those technology designers are starting to talk about moving beyond productivity. Let's face it: engineering is great for developing optimized solutions to problems, for figuring out how to get things done quickly and efficiently. But what it's not so good for is figuring out how technical solutions will fit into people's lives. What will be personally meaningful to me? How will a device resonate with my values? How will it alter the texture of my everyday life? Will this change be for the better? These are questions that technology designers are turning to the humanities to answer.

Take, for instance, my beloved robotic vacuum cleaner. Don't get me wrong — a robot taking over a dreaded household chore is a good thing. There's nothing like lying on the sofa and watching a robot take care of my personal business. And there's no doubt that this robot does what it is designed to do — it does a heck of a job getting the floor clean. But what does this mean for me, for my life, for my family?

Historians of technology have an answer. This answer is rooted in a depressing trend: despite social changes and a proliferation of time-saving gadgets, women are spending about the same amount of time on housework today as they did a century ago. Why is this? First, when gadgets make it easier to do a task around the home, standards for that task go up: now clothes should be cleaner, the bathroom should always sparkle, there should be home-made bread with dinner; tasks may be shorter but are done more often. Second, when tasks are automated, work tends to shift to other kinds of tasks. Housewives today don't need to pluck chickens any more, but they do have to spend time driving to the grocery store to get a conveniently plucked chicken. Third, there tends to be a trade-off in automation between saving time and saving labor — generally speaking, either you save time or you save work, but not both. Finally, time-saving gadgets have tended to streamline the work that men and children do, while often leaving women's work untouched — in the nineteenth century, men benefited from coal and central heat that eliminated the chore of wood-chopping, children benefited from central plumbing that eliminated the chore of water-carrying, while women's work was fairly untouched.

What does this have to do with robots doing our domestic chores today? Sadly, everything — at least at my house. Robotic vacuum cleaners change my standards: it's so easy to get the floor clean that I do it whenever it looks a bit dirty. They shift work from one task to another: instead of vacuuming, I'm now picking up things that the vacuum would choke on and rearranging the furniture so the robot doesn't get stuck. They do save me labor, but they don't save me time — it takes five times as long for the robot to do the job as a person. Finally, in my household at least, it does streamline men's labor, at the expense of women — it's my husband's job to do the vacuuming, but with the robot it's so easy that half the time I end up doing it instead. Despite its efficiency, in my life what a robotic vacuum means is that I clean more, I have new tasks, it takes longer to get done, and my husband is once again off the hook.

To put it another way, a household full of appliances that do things does not save time. It just does more. And more isn't necessarily better.

History of technology suggests that, in technology design, even if we're focused on usefulness, we should be asking some hard questions about what exactly usefulness means. What kinds of new labor is a "labor-saving" device creating? How should a particular device balance between saving time and saving labor? Who gets to save time, and who is overlooked? And, finally, shouldn't we be considering devices that don't save time at all but just make our lives better? What do we mean when we say we want a better life — besides checking more and more items off that to-do list?

Those answers don't come from engineering — they come from the humanities. And some technology designers are now drawing on these ideas to create new forms of everyday technology. They are shifting focus, designing technologies not for efficiency and for usefulness, but for fun, for pleasure, for curiosity, for daydreaming — for quality of life.

Consider the Drift Table, recently developed by interaction designer Bill Gaver and his team at Goldsmiths College at the University of London. This low-slung electronic coffee table comes equipped with a porthole displaying aerial views of the English countryside. As things are placed on the table, the landscape begins to slowly drift past the porthole in the direction of the heaviest objects. A trip across England could be made through the judicious placement of household objects and would run over the course of several days. Most of the time, though, the Drift Table is simply drifting on some random course, landscape lazily flowing by.

What is the Drift Table designed for? It is not designed as a tool to help you find your way across the United Kingdom; it is deliberately too slow and too hard to control to make using it to map the route to your friend's house in Brighton a pleasant prospect. Instead, it provides an invitation: as landscape lazily flows by the porthole, you are invited to let go of your desire to achieve just one more task and instead to drift, to dream, to enjoy.

We're thinking about these things at Cornell, too. Propped against the wall above my desk stands a large picture frame containing, apparently, a small drawing. Move closer to the picture, and you'll see that the "drawing" is actually video, displayed in a black-and-white, sketchy style. This video shows the neighboring office, populated by my good friend, Simeon. When I glance at this living sketch, I can't see exactly what Simeon is doing or who is visiting him, but I can tell whether he's there, whether he's socializing, and, based on how he moves, I can get a sense, too, of how he's feeling. Does Simeon want to take a break for a cup of coffee? A glance at the moving picture above my desk tells me if he might be in the mood.

This system, called Affector, is designed for work environments, but it's not designed for work. Instead, it supports the friendships that invisibly overlay the work space, highlights that we aren't just productivity machines, and suggests that having a background awareness of a friendly companion at work can be good for people and make them happy. Does Affector increase productivity? Are happier workers also more productive workers? Well, maybe, but the question isn't relevant. Improving quality of everyday life is worth striving for on its own, we believe, whether or not it helps us get more done.

So what does it take to build technologies that support these new kinds of values — open-ended curiosity, camaraderie, time for reflection, maybe even slowing down? It takes the humanities. They highlight for us the values that drive technology design and uncover the complex ways in which people make technologies personally meaningful in their everyday lives.

Ironically, then, one thing the humanities may be useful for is helping technology design out of the trap of usefulness. Engineering is great for optimizing utility, but, as it turns out, usefulness is not all it's cracked up to be. For learning not only how to do more, faster, but also how to do less, better, the humanities are an essential tool. Maybe one day we will speak of great technologies as being like the humanities — useless, and, therefore, good.

In Praise of Nuance

Shawkat Toorawa

I confess that, at first, I regarded the question "Do the Humanities Have to be Useful?" as something of an affront. My instinctive response was "Absolutely not! Why should they have to be useful? The humanities aren't about use or usefulness, they're about the life of the mind, about affect, about metaphor, about nuance, about sensibility!" Then I thought, "But those are useful. How and what would life be without them? It would surely be life without music, without poetry, without humor. Good grief!" And then it occurred to me that there are people, honorable people all, who do not see the humanities as useful. That if humanists do not respond, then non-humanists might respond for us. That it is altogether fitting and proper that we should do this.

A response in three parts, then.

Part 1. In praise of rhetoric

The humanities traditionally included rhetoric, the art of using language effectively and persuasively. They still do, principally because we must all be able to use language effectively and persuasively and because we must recognize when others do so and when others do not. If we ignore this, the liabilities are considerable: we risk taking things at face value, we risk being unmoved by pleas, we risk mistaking art for matter. And where would we be without allusion, without poetry, without wit, without dance, without song…without words?

Part 2. In praise of metaphor

Consider the following 100 words[1]:

> A dragon lives forever
> But not so little boys
> Painted wings and giant rings
> Make way for other toys.
>
> One grey night it happened,
> Jackie Paper came no more
> And Puff that mighty dragon,
> He ceased his fearless roar.
>
> His head was bent in sorrow,
> Green scales fell like rain,
> Puff no longer went to play
> Along the cherry lane.
>
> Without his life-long friend,
> Puff could not be brave,
> So Puff that mighty dragon
> Sadly slipped into his cave. Oh!
>
> Puff, the magic dragon
> Lived by the sea
> And frolicked in the autumn mist
> In a land called Honah Lee

Does a dragon live forever? Is a dragon a toy? What rings? What is a grey night? Is Puff an appropriate name for a mighty dragon? Do scales fall like rain? What is a cherry lane? More generally: What is the song about? What does it mean? How does it work?

The answers (possible ones, that is) are simple. Dragons don't live forever, but ideas do. The point isn't that the dragon is a toy but that when the boy grows up, the dragon is reduced to one of many simple (mechanical) distractions. Rings may be the pattern on the dragon, but they are also part of the rhythmic pattern of the song. A grey night is like a winter of discontent or an autumn of mellow fruitfulness. The name Puff is both childlike and ephemeral. No, scales do not fall like rain, but the image adumbrates tears and sadness. I don't know what a cherry lane is but both lanes and cherries are (in the American imagination) positive images. The song is about the loss of innocence. It is asking us not to let go of that innocence. It is about being human. It works by using or appealing to our ability to recognize:

• affect, affection, allusion, association;
• connotation;
• drift, essence, empathy, feeling, gist, hint, hue;
• intimation;
• meaning, metaphor;
• nuance, overtone, passion;
• persuasion;
• sense, sensibility, significance, spirit, symbol, tenor.

That capacity is a human one, a capacity to experience, produce, and comprehend language and expression, literature and rhetoric, art and aesthetics, history and perspective, desire and responsibility, music and improvisation, humor and wit — and to learn from all of them.

Part 3. In praise of nuance

Now consider the following passage[2]:

> *How many roads must a man walk down*
> *Before you call him a man?*
> *Yes, 'n' how many seas must a white dove sail*
> *Before she sleeps in the sand?*
> *Yes, 'n' how many times must the cannonballs fly*
> *Before they're forever banned?*
> *The answer, my friend, is blowin' in the wind,*
> *The answer is blowin' in the wind.*

Do the humanities have to be useful? The answer, my friend, is blowin' in the wind.

---

[1] "Puff the Magic Dragon," written by Peter Yarrow and Leonard Lipton © 1963 Pepamar Music Corp., first appears on Moving by Peter, Paul, and Mary, Warner Brothers Music, 1963.

[2] "Blowin' in the Wind," written by Bob Dylan (April 16, 1962), first appears on The Freewheelin' Bob Dylan © 1962 Columbia Records (renewed 1990, Special Rider Music).

About the Authors

Dominic Boyer is an assistant professor in the Department of Anthropology. He holds a bachelor's degree from Brown University (1992) and master's (1994) and PhD (2000) degrees from the University of Chicago. His research and teaching interests include: media, mediation, and public culture; intellectuals and the social formation of knowledge; language, identity, and social belonging; social and phenomenological analysis of professions and professionalism; journalism; anthropology, and sociology of Europe; East/West European relations; the social history of the German middle-classes; and dialectical philosophy. His current research project, The Practice of News Journalism in the Era of Global Informational Economies, analyzes the political-economic, social, and phenomenological dimensions of news journalism.

Ross Brann is the Milton R. Konvitz Professor of Judeo-Islamic Studies, chair of the Department of Near Eastern Studies, and Alice H. Cook House Professor and Dean. He holds a PhD from New York University (1981). His books include *The Compunctious Poet: Cultural Ambiguity and Hebrew Poetry in Muslim Spain* (Johns Hopkins University Press, 1991), recipient of the 1992 National Jewish Book Award in Sephardic Studies, and *Power in the Portrayal: Representations of Jews and Muslims in Eleventh- and Twelfth-Century Islamic Spain* (Princeton University Press, 2002). Brann joined the Cornell faculty in 1986. He has received a John S. Guggenheim Memorial Foundation Fellowship and three National Endowment for the Humanities fellowships and was awarded the Stephen and Margery Russell Distinguished Teaching Award in 1996.

Laura Brown is the John Wendell Anderson Professor of English. She holds a bachelor's degree from Stanford University (1971) and a PhD from the University of California, Berkeley (1977). Her scholarly interests include Restoration and eighteenth-century English literature, especially matters of generic history, ideology, and form; feminist criticism; Marxist criticism and cultural critique. Her publications include *English Dramatic Form 1660–1760: An Essay in Generic History* (Yale University Press, 1981), *Alexander Pope in Rereading Literature* (Oxford, 1985), and *The New Eighteenth Century: Theory, Politics, English Literature*, edited with Felicity Nussbaum (Methuen, 1987), and *Ends of Empire: Women and Ideology in Early Eighteenth-Century English Literature* (Cornell University Press, 1993).

Walter Cohen is a professor of comparative literature and a faculty fellow in Cornell's Society for the Humanities. He holds a bachelor's degree from Stanford University (1971) and master's (1974) and PhD (1980) degrees from the University of California, Berkeley. He has written *Drama of a Nation: Public Theater in Renaissance England and Spain* (Cornell University Press, 1985) and is one of four co-editors of *The Norton Shakespeare* (1997). He is completing a book, *The Literature of Europe and the West*, and the second edition of *The Norton Shakespeare*. He previously served as vice provost and dean of the Graduate School.

Katherine Crocker is a Cornell undergraduate with dual majors in chemistry and chemical biology and English. She will graduate in 2008.

Jonathan Culler is the Class of 1916 Professor of English and Comparative Literature. He holds a bachelor's degree (summa cum laude) from Harvard University (1966) and two DPhil degrees (1968 and 1972) from St. John's College, Oxford University. He has worked on nineteenth-century French literature (especially on Flaubert and Baudelaire) and on contemporary literary theory and criticism (especially structuralism, deconstruction, and French theory generally). He teaches courses on literary theory and on aspects of the history of the lyric. His best-known works are *Flaubert: The Uses of Uncertainty, Structuralist Poetics, Roland Barthes, Ferdinand de Saussure, On Deconstruction*, and *Literary Theory: A Very Short Introduction*. He is completing a term as president of the American Comparative Literature Association.

Brett de Bary is professor of Asian studies and comparative literature and is director of the Society for the Humanities. She holds a bachelor's degree from Barnard College and a PhD from Harvard University (1978). She specializes in modern Japanese literature and film and is former director of the Visual Studies program. She is an associate editor of *Traces: Multilingual Series of Translation and Cultural Theory* and has published criticism and translations in the areas of Japanese fiction, film, feminist criticism, and post-modern theory. She has published essays and translations on postwar Japanese literature, feminism, and critical theory, including editing "Gender and Imperialism" (*U.S.-Japan Women's Journal*, 1997). She co-edited the *Traces* special issue "'Race' Panic and the Memory of Migration" (2002).

Jane Fajans is associate professor of anthropology. She holds a bachelor's degree (1971) from Bryn Mawr College and a PhD (1985) from Stanford University. Her scholarly interests include the anthropology of food, symbolic anthropology, oceania, work, personhood, social and cultural anthropology, ritual and symbolic forms, socialization, and life cycle and gender studies. She received the Robert and Helen Appel Fellowship for Humanists and Social Scientists in 1997. She serves as advisor to the Singapore Students Association. She is author of *They Make Themselves: Work and Play among the Baining of Papua New Guinea* (University of Chicago Press, 1997).

David Feldshuh is professor of theater and has served as artistic director of the Schwartz Center for the Performing Arts since 1984. He holds a bachelor's degree from Dartmouth College and PhD and MD degrees from the University of Minnesota. His play, *Miss Evers' Boys*, about the Tuskegee syphilis study, has been produced throughout the United States, received the New American Play award, was nominated for the Pulitzer Prize, and won seven Emmy awards as an HBO movie. His short story "Are You Satisfied, Thomas Becket?" was recently published in a collection of stories by physician-writers. He continues to practice medicine and lectures frequently on the subject of human experimentation and the use of theatre in exploring important social issues.

Salah Hassan is associate professor of African and African Diaspora art history and visual culture and is director of the Africana Studies and Research Center. He holds a bachelor's degree from the University of Khartoum (1978) and master's (1984) and PhD (1988) degrees from the University of Pennsylvania. He is founder and editor of *NKA: Journal of Contemporary African Art* and serves as consulting editor for *African Arts* and *Atlantica*. His books include *Unpacking Europe* (2001) *Authentic/Ex-Centric: Conceptualism in Contemporary African Art* (2001), *Gendered Visions: The Art of Contemporary Africana Women Artists* (1997) and *Art and Islamic Literacy Among the Hausa of Northern Nigeria* (1992).

Peter Uwe Hohendahl is the Jacob Gould Schurman Professor of German and Comparative Literature and director of the Institute for German Cultural Studies. He holds a doctorate from Hamburg University (1964). He was elected to the American Academy of Arts and Sciences in 2003. He has written articles on Adorno, Benn, Börne, Dilthey, Fontane, Habermas, Heine, Lukács and Stifter; the eighteenth-century novel, literary criticism, East German literature, and critical theory. His books include *Das Bild der bürgerlichen Welt im expressionistischen Drama*; *Gottfried Benn: Wirkung wider Willen*; *Literaturkritik und Offentlichkeit*; *Der europäische Roman der Empfindsamkeit*; *The Institution of Criticism*; *Literarische Kultur im Zeitalter des Liberalismus, 1830–1870*; and *Building a National Literature: The Case of Germany, 1830–1870*.

Biodun Jeyifo is a professor of English. He holds a bachelor's degree from the University of Ibadan (1970) and master's (1973) and PhD (1975) degrees from New York University. He has written books and monographs on African and African-American theatre and drama, on the entire oeuvre of Wole Soyinka, and on colonial studies and postcolonial critical theory. His areas of research include comparative post-coloniality, Marxist cultural theory, film and popular culture and twentieth-century revolutionary social philosophy. He served as associate chair of the Department of English from 2002–2005 and as editorial board member of *Diacritics and Transition*.

Rayna Kalas is an assistant professor of English. She holds a bachelor's degree from the University of Chicago (1990) and a PhD from the University of Pennsylvania (2000). Her scholarly interests include sixteenth- and seventeenth-century poetry and prose; Renaissance drama; literature and the visual arts; criticism and theory; historicist and materialist literary criticism; literature and technology; and theories of labor and literary production. Her publications include "The Technology of Reflection: Renaissance Mirrors of Steel and Glass," *Journal of Medieval and Early Modern Studies* 32 (2002) and "The Language of Framing," *Shakespeare Studies* 28 (2000).

Dominick LaCapra is professor of history and the Bryce and Edith M. Bowmar Professor in Humanistic Studies and was the director of the Society for the Humanities. He holds a bachelor's degree from Cornell University (1961) and master's (1963) and PhD (1970) degrees from Harvard University. His books include *Writing History, Writing Trauma* (Johns Hopkins University Press, 2001), *History in Transit: Experience, Identity, Critical Theory* (Cornell University Press, 2004) and *History and Reading: Tocqueville, Foucault, French Studies* (University of Toronto Press, 2000). He received the Award for Aesthetic Theory from the Dactyl Foundation and an Institutional Grant from the Mellon Foundation for program enhancement at the Society for the Humanities, both in 2001.

G. Peter Lepage is the Harold Tanner Dean of the College of Arts and Sciences and professor of physics. He holds a bachelor's degree from McGill University and master's (1975) and PhD (1978) degrees from Stanford University. A theoretical particle physicist whose recent research has focused on numerical simulations of quantum field theories, Lepage joined the Cornell faculty in 1980 and has spent his entire professorial career as a physicist. He has had visiting appointments at the Institute for Nuclear Theory, the Fermi National Accelerator Laboratory, the Institute for Theoretical Physics, the Department of Applied Mathematics and Theoretical Physics at the University of Cambridge, and the Institute for Advanced Study in Princeton. He received a John Simon Guggenheim Fellowship in 1996–1997 and an Alfred P. Sloan Fellowship in 1990.

Rose Ellen Lessy is a graduate student in the Department of English.

Carolyn (Biddy) Martin is university provost and professor of German studies. She holds a PhD (1985) in German literature from the University of Wisconsin-Madison and joined the Cornell faculty in 1984. She chaired the Department of German Studies from 1994–1997 and in 1997 was promoted to full professor. In 1996 she was appointed senior associate dean in the College of Arts and Sciences and became provost in 2000. Her publications include *Woman and Modernity: The (Life) Styles of Lou Andreas-Salome* (Cornell University Press, 1991) and *Femininity Played Straight* (Routledge Press, 1996). Martin is a member of the national steering committee on the humanities organized by the Association of American Universities and the American Council of Learned Societies and is charged with initiating and developing strategies to examine the role and status of the humanities.

Mohsen Mostafavi, the Arthur L. and Isabel B. Wiesenberger Professor in Architecture, was named dean of the College of Architecture, Art, and Planning in 2004. He attended Clare Hall, Cambridge University, the University of Essex and the London Architectural Association School of Architecture (AA). He served two successful terms as chairman of the AA, London's leading school of architecture, and directed the Master of Architecture 1 Program at Harvard University's Graduate School of Design. A member of the Royal Institute of British Architects, his recent publications include: *Approximations* (AA/MIT, 2002); *Surface Architecture* (MIT, 2002), which received the CICA Bruno Zevi Book Award; *Logique Visuelle* (Idea Books, 2003); and *Landscape Urbanism: A Manual for the Machinic Landscape* (AA Publications, 2004). Mostafavi is Cornell's university liaison to the Association of American University/American Council of Learned Societies' national steering committee on the humanities.

Phoebe Sengers is an assistant professor of information science and science and technology studies. She holds a PhD from Carnegie Mellon University (1998). From 1999–2001, she performed research in agents, avatars, virtual environments, and computer graphics in the Media Arts Research Studies group at the GMD Institute for Media Communication in Bonn, Germany. She has been active in the narrative intelligence research community and in 1998–1999 was a Fulbright Guest Researcher at the Center for Art and Media Technology (ZKM) in Karlsruhe, Germany. Her PhD was the result of a self-defined interdisciplinary program in artificial intelligence and cultural theory administered by the Department of Computer Science and the Program in Literary and Cultural Theory.

Shawkat Toorawa is an assistant professor of Arabic literature and Islamic studies and director of graduate studies in the Department of Near Eastern Studies. He holds bachelor's (1985), master's (1989), and PhD (1998) degrees from the University of Pennsylvania. His interests are classical and medieval Arabic literature, modern Arabic poetry, plural Islam, and the Indian Ocean. He is co-author of *Interpreting the Self: Autobiography in the Arabic Literary Tradition* (University of California Press, 2001), translator of Adonis's *A Time Between Ashes and Roses* (Syracuse University Press, 2004), co-editor of *Law and Education in Medieval Islam: Studies in Memory of George Makdisi* (Gibb Trust, 2004), and author of *Ibn Abi Tahir Tayfur and Arabic Writerly Culture: A ninth-century bookman in Baghdad* (RoutledgeCurzon, 2005).